Human Body Experiments

FACTS ON FILE SCIENCE EXPERIMENTS

Human Body Experiments

Pamela Walker
Elaine Wood

Facts On File
An imprint of Infobase Publishing

Human Body Experiments

Facts On File, Inc.
An imprint of Infobase Publishing
132 West 31st Street
New York NY 10001

Library of Congress Cataloging-in-Publication Data
Walker, Pam, 1958-
Human body experiments / Pamela Walker, Elaine Wood.
p. cm.—(Facts on File Science experiments)
Includes bibliographical references and index.
ISBN 978-0-8160-8171-4
1. Anatomy–Experiments–Juvenile literature. 2. Anatomy–Study and teaching (Middle school)–Activity programs. 3. Anatomy–Study and teaching (Secondary)–Activity programs.
I. Wood, Elaine, 1950- II. Title.
QL806.5.W35 2011
612.0078–dc22
2010011138

Facts On File books are available at special discounts when purchased in bulk quantities for businesses, associations, institutions, or sales promotions. Please call our Special Sales Department in New York at (212) 967-8800 or (800) 322-8755.

You can find Facts On File on the World Wide Web at http://www.factsonfile.com

All links and Web addresses were checked and verified to be correct at the time of publication. Because of the dynamic nature of the Web, some addresses and links may have changed since publication and may no longer be valid.

Editor: Frank K. Darmstadt
Copy Editor: Betsy Feist at A Good Thing, Inc.
Project Coordinator: Aaron Richman
Art Director: Howard Petlack
Production: Victoria Kessler
Illustrations: Hadel Studios
Cover printed by: Bang Printing, Brainerd, MN
Book printed and bound by Bang Printing, Brainerd, MN
Date printed: September 2010
Printed in the United States of America

10 9 8 7 6 5 4 3 2 1

This book is printed on acid-free paper.

Contents

Preface

For centuries, humans have studied and explored the natural world around them. The ever-growing body of knowledge resulting from these efforts is science. Information gained through science is passed from one generation to the next through an array of educational programs. One of the primary goals of every science education program is to help young people develop critical-thinking and problem-solving skills that they can use throughout their lives.

Science education is unique in academics in that it not only conveys facts and skills; it also cultivates curiosity and creativity. For this reason, science is an active process that cannot be fully conveyed by passive teaching techniques. The question for educators has always been, "What is the best way to teach science?" There is no simple answer to this question, but studies in education provide useful insights.

Research indicates that students need to be actively involved in science, learning it through experience. Science students are encouraged to go far beyond the textbook and to ask questions, consider novel ideas, form their own predictions, develop experiments or procedures, collect information, record results, analyze findings, and use a variety of resources to expand knowledge. In other words, students cannot just hear science; they must also do science.

"Doing" science means performing experiments. In the science curriculum, experiments play a number of educational roles. In some cases, hands-on activities serve as hooks to engage students and introduce new topics. For example, a discrepant event used as an introductory experiment encourages questions and inspires students to seek the answers behind their findings. Classroom investigations can also help expand information that was previously introduced or cement new knowledge. According to neuroscience, experiments and other types of hands-on learning help transfer new learning from short-term into long-term memory.

Facts On File Science Experiments is a multivolume set of experiments that helps engage students and enable them to "do" science. The high-interest experiments in these books put students' minds into gear and give them opportunities to become involved, to think independently, and to build on their own base of science knowledge.

As a resource, Facts On File Science Experiments provides teachers with new and innovative classroom investigations that are presented in a clear, easy-to-understand style. The areas of study in the multivolume set include forensic science, environmental science, computer research, physical science, and space and astronomy as well as many other subjects. Experiments are supported by colorful figures and line illustrations that help hold students' attention and explain information. All of the experiments in these books use multiple science process skills such as observing, measuring, classifying, analyzing, and predicting. In addition, some of the experiments require students to practice inquiry science by setting up and carrying out their own open-ended experiments.

Each volume of the set contains 20 new experiments as well as extensive safety guidelines, glossary, correlation to the National Science Education Standards, scope and sequence, and an annotated list of Internet resources. An introduction that presents background information begins each investigation to provide an overview of the topic. Every experiment also includes relevant specific safety tips along with materials list, procedure, analysis questions, explanation of the experiment, connections to real life, and an annotated further reading section for extended research.

Pam Walker and Elaine Wood, the authors of Facts On File Science Experiments, are sensitive to the needs of both science teachers and students. The writing team has more than 40 years of combined science teaching experience. Both are actively involved in planning and improving science curricula in their home state, Georgia, where Pam was the 2007 Teacher of the Year. Walker and Wood are master teachers who hold specialist degrees in science and science education. They are the authors of dozens of books for middle and high school science teachers and students.

Facts On File Science Experiments, by Walker and Wood, facilitates science instruction by making it easy for teachers to incorporate experimentation. During experiments, students reap benefits that are not available in other types of instruction. One of these benefits is the opportunity to take advantage of the learning provided by social interactions. Experiments are usually carried out in small groups, enabling students to brainstorm and learn from each other. The validity of group work as an effective learning tool is supported by research in neuroscience, which shows that the brain is a social organ and that communication and collaboration are activities that naturally enhance learning.

Experimentation addresses many different types of learning, including lateral thinking, multiple intelligences, and constructivism. In lateral thinking, students solve problems using nontraditional methods. Long-established, rigid procedures for problem-solving are replaced by original ideas from students.

When encouraged to think laterally, students are more likely to come up with unique ideas that are not usually found in the traditional classroom. This type of thinking requires students to construct meaning from an activity and to think like scientists.

Another benefit of experimentation is that it accommodates students' multiple intelligences. According to the theory of multiple intelligences, students possess many different aptitudes, but in varying degrees. Some of these forms of intelligence include linguistic, musical, logical-mathematical, spatial, kinesthetic, intrapersonal, and interpersonal. Learning is more likely to be acquired and retained when more than one sense is involved. During an experiment, students of all intellectual types find roles in which they can excel.

Students in the science classroom become involved in active learning, constructing new ideas based on their current knowledge and their experimental findings. The constructivist theory of learning encourages students to discover principles for and by themselves. Through problem solving and independent thinking, students build on what they know, moving forward in a manner that makes learning real and lasting.

Active, experimental learning makes connections between newly acquired information and the real world, a world that includes jobs. In the 21st century, employers expect their employees to identify and solve problems for themselves. Therefore, today's students, workers of the near future, will be required to use higher-level thinking skills. Experience with science experiments provides potential workers with the ability and confidence to be problem solvers.

The goal of Walker and Wood in this multivolume set is to provide experiments that hook and hold the interest of students, teach basic concepts of science, and help students develop their critical-thinking skills. When fully immersed in an experiment, students can experience those "Aha!" moments, the special times when new information merges with what is already known and understanding breaks through. On these occasions, real and lasting learning takes place. The authors hope that this set of books helps bring more "Aha" moments into every science class.

Acknowledgments

This book would not exist were it not for our editor, Frank K. Darmstadt, who conceived and directed the project. Frank supervised the material closely, editing and making invaluable comments along the way. Betsy Feist of A Good Thing, Inc., is responsible for transforming our raw material into a polished and grammatically correct manuscript that makes us proud.

Introduction

Instructors of courses on the human body have an advantage over those in many other disciplines because students are curious about how their own bodies work. For this reason, the study of the human body can be very personal and relevant to students' lives. The study can develop students' curiosity and get them to thinking about what happens when the body does not function properly. Because students are already motivated to learn about the topics in the course, they are able to synthesize abstract concepts and relate them to real events.

The study of the human body can be a rigorous course, introducing hundreds of new terms and complex structures. In many cases, students memorize the terms they need to know for a test. However, memorization does not equal learning; memorized material is only stored in the short-term memory. A much better way to learn the subject is by doing it, experiencing human anatomy and physiology from an interactive approach. This enables students to see how one structure works with another, giving meaning to the extensive terminology and making the material applicable.

Once students are engaged in the topics of the human body, they have plenty of questions. Comments might range from simple ones such as, "One time I had a strange bump on my skin. What do you think it is?" to very complex problems such as "My MRI showed a swollen duct in my pancreas, and I was wondering what that means." At this level of engagement, instruction becomes important to students because it provides them with information they need.

The study of the human body includes both anatomy (the physical structures) and physiology (the way these structures function). In schools, human body science is introduced on the elementary or middle school level and is extended into postgraduate work. At each level, students benefit from meaningful experiences. In *Human Body Experiments*, middle and high school science teachers have 20 original experiments to supplement and support their course. *Human Body Experiments* is one volume of the new Facts On File Science Experiments set.

The experiments in this book can be taught in any order. Several lessons enable students to understand the functions of support systems and analyze the interdependence of muscle, skeleton, and integument. These lessons include "Tissues in the Human Body," "External Anatomy of the Fetal Pig," "The Integumentary System," "Bone and Cartilage Structure," "Types of Muscles," and "Vertebrae of the Neck." The first three of these lessons center on the four major types of tissues, with the primary focus on epithelial tissues and their derivatives. The last three emphasize the way structures of the skeletal system provide support and the how these structures work with muscle to enable us to move.

The human body's movements, behaviors, and responses are coordinated by two systems, the endocrine and nervous systems. Nerves and endocrine secretions interact to provide smooth, coordinated actions. "Dissection of a Cow's Eye," and "Meissner's Corpuscles in Skin" help students understand how the body perceives stimuli and converts them into information that can be processed by the brain. "Reaction Time" is an experiment that demonstrates how the brain can be distracted from one task by another.

The respiratory, immune, cardiovascular, digestive, and urinary systems work together to accomplish transportation, absorption, and excretion. The cardiovascular system, made up of the heart, vessels, and blood, distributes a variety of materials around the body. In "Model of the Heart," students analyze the heart's function and structure by creating a model. "Diagnosis of Blood Diseases" provides information on normal blood cells and blood counts and shows what happens when abnormalities develop. The environment of blood cells is explored in "Osmosis in Red Blood Cells." In two experiments, "What Factors Affect Blood Pressure?" and "Exercise, Pulse, and Recovery Rate," students learn how their heart and vessels function together to keep adequate supplies of blood flowing through the body.

Blood carries digested food to cells. Students show the gross anatomy of the structures involved in food break down in "Model of the Digestive System." The chemical characteristics of different foods are explored in "Food Analysis." The role of lactase in the digestive system is studied in "Lactose Intolerance." In "Urinalysis," students find out what kind of information can be gathered from urine.

Students of the human body also learn how the male and female reproductive systems produce gametes and regulate fertility with hormones. In "Male Reproductive System" and "Female Reproductive System," students examine histological structures of both systems and relate these structures to their functions.

Many educators feel that the most valuable classroom experiences are inquiry experiments, those that push students out of their comfort zones and require them to synthesize products based on their knowledge. One way to accomplish this goal is to have students develop their own experimental ideas or create their own experimental procedures to solve a problem. Experiments in this book that require students to develop part or all of an experimental procedure include "Food Analysis," "Osmosis in Red Blood Cells," "Reaction Time," "Exercise, Pulse, and Recovery Rate," and "Meissner's Corpuscles in Skin." Two other experiments require independent thought and assimilation of concepts, "Model of the Heart" and "Model of the Digestive System."

The authors of *Human Body Experiments* hope that teachers will find a wide variety of lessons in this book that help them convey key concepts to their students. One of our primary goals is to make experimentation in the classroom easy and productive for the teacher. The other goal is to see students become excited and engaged in the study of the human body.

Safety Precautions

REVIEW BEFORE STARTING ANY EXPERIMENT

Each experiment includes special safety precautions that are relevant to that particular project. These do not include all the basic safety precautions that are necessary whenever you are working on a scientific experiment. For this reason, it is absolutely necessary that you read and remain mindful of the General Safety Precautions that follow. Experimental science can be dangerous and good laboratory procedure always includes following basic safety rules. Things can happen quickly while you are performing an experiment—for example, materials can spill, break, or even catch on fire. There will not be time after the fact to protect yourself. Always prepare for unexpected dangers by following the basic safety guidelines during the entire experiment, whether or not something seems dangerous to you at a given moment.

We have been quite sparing in prescribing safety precautions for the individual experiments. For one reason, we want you to take very seriously the safety precautions that are printed in this book. If you see it written here, you can be sure that it is here because it is absolutely critical.

Read the safety precautions here and at the beginning of each experiment before performing each lab activity. It is difficult to remember a long set of general rules. By rereading these general precautions every time you set up an experiment, you will be reminding yourself that lab safety is critically important. In addition, use your good judgment and pay close attention when performing potentially dangerous procedures. Just because the book does not say "Be careful with hot liquids" or "Don't cut yourself with a knife" does not mean that you can be careless when boiling water or using a knife to punch holes in plastic bottles. Notes in the text are special precautions to which you must pay special attention.

GENERAL SAFETY PRECAUTIONS

Accidents can be caused by carelessness, haste, or insufficient knowledge. By practicing safety procedures and being alert while conducting experiments, you can avoid taking an unnecessary risk. Be sure to check the individual experiments in this book for additional safety regulations and adult supervision requirements. If you will be working in a laboratory, do not work alone. When you are working off site, keep in groups with a minimum of three students per group, and follow school rules and state legal requirements for the number of supervisors required. Ask an adult supervisor with basic training in first aid to carry a small first-aid kit. Make sure everyone knows where this person will be during the experiment.

PREPARING

- Clear all surfaces before beginning experiments.
- Read the entire experiment before you start.
- Know the hazards of the experiments and anticipate dangers.

PROTECTING YOURSELF

- Follow the directions step by step.
- Perform only one experiment at a time.
- Locate exits, fire blanket and extinguisher, master gas and electricity shut-offs, eyewash, and first-aid kit.
- Make sure there is adequate ventilation.
- Do not participate in horseplay.
- Do not wear open-toed shoes.
- Keep floor and workspace neat, clean, and dry.
- Clean up spills immediately.
- If glassware breaks, do not clean it up by yourself; ask for teacher assistance.
- Tie back long hair.
- Never eat, drink, or smoke in the laboratory or workspace.
- Do not eat or drink any substances tested unless expressly permitted to do so by a knowledgeable adult.

USING EQUIPMENT WITH CARE

- Set up apparatus far from the edge of the desk.
- Use knives or other sharp, pointed instruments with care.

- Pull plugs, not cords, when removing electrical plugs.

- Clean glassware before and after use.

- Check glassware for scratches, cracks, and sharp edges.

- Let your teacher know about broken glassware immediately.

- Do not use reflected sunlight to illuminate your microscope.

- Do not touch metal conductors.

- Take care when working with any form of electricity.

- Use alcohol-filled thermometers, not mercury-filled thermometers.

USING CHEMICALS

- Never taste or inhale chemicals.

- Label all bottles and apparatus containing chemicals.

- Read labels carefully.

- Avoid chemical contact with skin and eyes (wear safety glasses or goggles, lab apron, and gloves).

- Do not touch chemical solutions.

- Wash hands before and after using solutions.

- Wipe up spills thoroughly.

HEATING SUBSTANCES

- Wear safety glasses or goggles, apron, and gloves when heating materials.

- Keep your face away from test tubes and beakers.

- When heating substances in a test tube, avoid pointing the top of the test tube toward other people.

- Use test tubes, beakers, and other glassware made of Pyrex™ glass.

- Never leave apparatus unattended.

- Use safety tongs and heat-resistant gloves.

- If your laboratory does not have heatproof workbenches, put your Bunsen burner on a heatproof mat before lighting it.

- Take care when lighting your Bunsen burner; light it with the airhole closed and use a Bunsen burner lighter rather than wooden matches.

- Turn off hot plates, Bunsen burners, and gas when you are done.
- Keep flammable substances away from flames and other sources of heat.
- Have a fire extinguisher on hand.

FINISHING UP

- Thoroughly clean your work area and any glassware used.
- Wash your hands.
- Be careful not to return chemicals or contaminated reagents to the wrong containers.
- Do not dispose of materials in the sink unless instructed to do so.
- Clean up all residues and put in proper containers for disposal.
- Dispose of all chemicals according to all local, state, and federal laws.

BE SAFETY CONSCIOUS AT ALL TIMES!

1. Tissues in the Human Body

Topic

The structures of the cells that make up tissues are determined by the functions of those tissues.

Introduction

The human body is made up of *tissues*, groups of similar cells performing the same functions. Tissues can be divided into four main types: connective, epithelial, nerve, and muscle. Each type of tissue has unique characteristics.

Connective tissue, the largest category, holds together and supports body systems. All connective tissue is made up of an extracellular, nonliving matrix, strong fibers, and cells. Blood is one type of connective tissue. The extracellular *matrix* in blood is plasma. Cells in blood include erythrocytes, leukocytes, and platelets. The fibers in blood do not form unless clotting is taking place. Bone, another type of connective tissue, has a strong extracellular matrix made up of calcium salts and collagen fibers. The cells in bone live in small cavities called *lacunae*. Other types of connective tissue include dense, loose, areolar, and cartilage.

Epithelial tissue protects us from the outside environment and lines our organs. Skin, glands, and membranes are some examples of epithelial tissue. Epithelial cells have two distinct surfaces: the *basal surface* and the free or *apical surface*. Adjacent cells are held closely together by special junctions.

Nerve tissue transmits signals as electrical impulses. A nerve cell, or *neuron*, has a central body and two or more extensions. The central body contains the nucleus and most of the organelles. Examples of nerve tissue are peripheral nerves, the brain, and the spinal cord.

Muscle tissue can contract and is responsible for movement. Three types of muscle tissue are cardiac muscle, smooth muscle, and skeletal muscle. Cardiac and smooth tissue contract without any thought on our part, so are considered to be *involuntary*. Skeletal tissue, on the other hand, is *voluntary* because we can contract it at will. Cardiac and skeletal muscle can be differentiated from smooth by their distinct striations.

In this experiment, you will examine slides of all four types of tissue.

Time Required

55 minutes

Materials

- light microscope
- colored pencils
- prepared slide of smooth muscle
- prepared slide of skeletal muscle
- prepared slide of cardiac muscle
- prepared slide of blood
- prepared slide of spinal cord (cross section)
- anatomy book or access to Internet sites on characteristics of tissues
- science notebook

Safety Note   Please review and follow the safety guidelines at the beginning of this volume.

Procedure

1. Observe smooth muscle tissue on low, medium, and high powers. Compare the slide to pictures in your anatomy book or to pictures of smooth muscle on the Internet.
2. In your science notebook, draw a view of smooth muscle as seen on high power. Use colored pencils to shade your drawing.
3. Label the nuclei of several smooth muscle cells.
4. Repeat steps 1 through 3 for skeletal muscle tissue and for cardiac muscle tissue. In these tissues, also label the striations.
5. Answer Analysis questions 1 and 2.

6. Observe a blood smear on low, medium, and high. Compare the slide to pictures in your anatomy book or to pictures of blood on the Internet. In your science notebook, draw each *formed element* (red blood cells, white blood cells, and platelets) as seen on high power. Label the nuclei of several white blood cells.

7. Answer Analysis question 3.

8. Observe the slide of spinal cord under low, medium, and high powers of your microscope. Compare the slide to pictures in your anatomy book or to pictures of spinal cord on the Internet.

   a. Describe the general appearance of the slide in your science notebook.

   b. Compare cells in the region that is pale to the cells in the other regions. Find two different star-shaped nerve cells. Draw the cells on medium or high in your science notebook. Label the nuclei.

   c. The central canal is a small hole in the middle of the spinal cord section. Look at the cells lining the central canal of the spinal cord. Draw these cells in your science notebook.

9. Answer Analysis questions 4 and 5.

10. Examine Figures 1, 2, 3, and 4. Compare each of the figures to photographs of these tissues in your anatomy book or to pictures of these tissues on the Internet. In your science notebook, give a brief description of each tissue.

11. Answer the Analysis question 6.

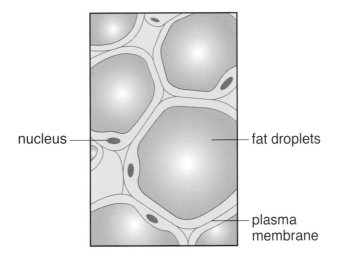

Figure 1

Adipose tissue is made up of fat cells. Each cell has a nucleus and plasma membrane. Fat droplets are stored within vacuoles inside the cells.

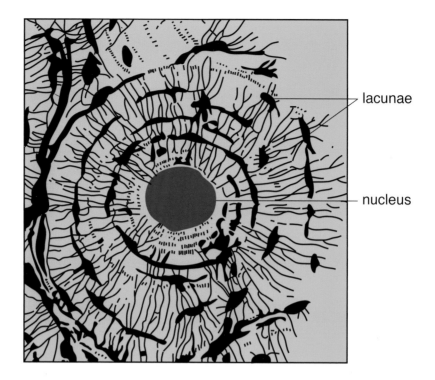

Figure 2

Bone cells live within the lacunae, small cavities in the mineral matrix.

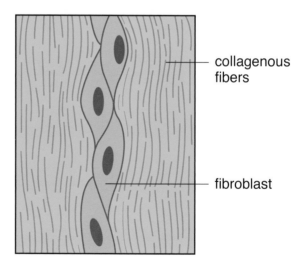

Figure 3

Dense connective tissue is made up of layers of collagenous fibers that are interspersed with fibroblasts.

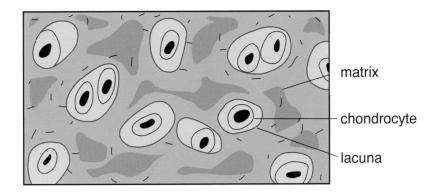

Figure 4

Hyaline cartilage is made up of a tough matrix that contains cells within lacunae.

Analysis

1. Skeletal and cardiac muscle are both striated. How can you tell them apart?

2. Complete the data table.

Data Table			
Muscle tissue type	**Striated or unstriated?**	**Voluntary or involuntary?**	**Example of location in body**
Skeletal			
Smooth			
Cardiac			

3. Are the nuclei of all white blood cells the same shape?

4. Describe the general shape and appearance of the spinal cord.

5. What type of cells lines the central canal of the spinal cord?

6. Match the following.

a. adipose tissue	**i.** gives elasticity to organs
b. bone	**ii.** matrix is hard and porous
c. blood	**iii.** contractile tissue in organs
d. cartilage	**iv.** fat
e. dense connective tissue	**v.** found in joints, nose, respiratory tract
f. smooth muscle	**vi.** matrix is plasma
g. skeletal muscle	**vii.** contractile tissue attached to bone
h. cardiac muscle	**viii.** contractile tissue in heart

What's Going On?

Cells are highly specialized for their functions. The jobs of epithelial tissue include protection, absorption, filtration, and secretion. Types of epithelial tissue are classified by the number of cell layers and by the shape of cells. One layer of epithelial cells is described as *simple* while multiple layers are *stratified*. The cells can be squamous cube-shaped, or columnar. Simple squamous epithelium is thin and flat and lines the air sacs in the lungs. Stratified squamous epithelium (Figure 5) is made of many layers and is found in our mouth and makes up our skin.

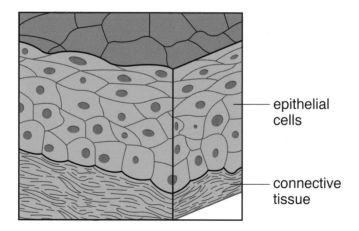

epithelial cells

connective tissue

Figure 5

Stratified squamous epithelium is made of several layers of epithelial cells.

Some epithelial cells display further modifications. In the trachea, epithelial cells are crowned with *cilia*, short, hairlike extensions that sweep material up toward the mouth and away from the lungs. The apical surface of epithelial cells in the small intestine is extensively folded to form *microvilli*, which increase the absorptive area of the cells. Epithelial cells that make up the skin produce keratin, a tough protein that helps protect the cells.

Connections

If damaged, some tissues can repair themselves through the process of *regeneration*. For example, if epithelial cells are scratched off of your knee, existing cells divide and produce new epithelial cells to repair the scratch. Fibrous connective tissue and bone tissue can do the same. Skeletal muscle can regenerate to some degree, but does so slowly. Nerve tissue, on the other hand, is not able to regenerate. Neurons are described as *amitotic*, meaning that they cannot undergo cell division. Therefore neurons that are damaged and lost cannot be replaced.

Want to Know More?

See appendix for Our Findings.

Further Reading

"Histology," November 9, 2006. Available online. URL: http://www.colorado.edu/intphys/iphy3415/histology/index.html. Accessed October 4, 2009. Labeled slides of integument, bone, muscle, digestive, circulatory, and nervous system tissues are on this Web site.

"Lumen," January 23, 2005. Loyola University Chicago Stritch School of Medicine. Available online. URL: http://www.meddean.luc.edu/LUMEN/MedEd/Histo/frames/histo_frames.html. Accessed October 4, 2009. Slides of human tissues, and explanations of the slides, can be found on this Web site.

Slomianka, Lutz. "Blue Histology," July 8, 2009. School of Anatomy and Human Biology, University of Western Australia. Available online. URL: http://www.lab.anhb.uwa.edu.au/mb140/. Accessed October 4, 2009. This extensive Web site provides information on each type of tissue as well as photographs of tissues under the light microscope.

2. External Anatomy of the Fetal Pig

Topic

The external anatomy of a fetal pig is similar to the external anatomy of humans.

Introduction

Like humans, pigs are *mammals* whose bodies are covered with hair and whose young are raised on milk produced by mammary glands. Most mammals, including pigs and humans, develop in a *placenta*, a structure that connects the developing embryo to the mother's uterus by way of an *umbilical cord* (see Figure 1). The length of *gestation*, the time it takes a fetal pig to complete development, is about 115 days.

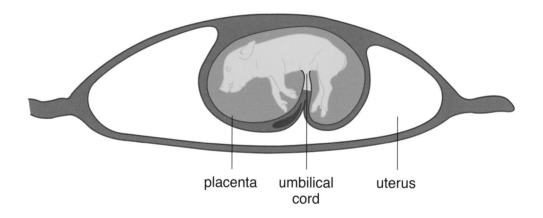

Figure 1

Cross section of a sow's abdomen showing the developing fetus, umbilical cord, and placenta.

Development gets under way when the egg of a female pig is released from the *ovary* and starts traveling down the *oviduct*. If the egg is fertilized, it undergoes cell division. By the sixth day of development, the cells start to specialize, and on day 11 the ball of cells attaches to the uterine lining. The solid ball of cells continues to change until it forms three distinct cell layers: the *endoderm*, *mesoderm*, and *ectoderm*. The endoderm develops into the digestive tract and lungs; the mesoderm forms the major organs; and the ectoderm becomes the skin and nervous system. In this experiment, you are going to examine the skin and other external structures of a fetal pig.

Time Required

55 minutes

Materials

- fetal pig
- gloves
- goggles
- masking tape
- dissection tray
- 20 dissection pins
- metric ruler
- paper towels
- science notebook

Safety Note   Take care when working with the preservative solution in which fetal pigs are embalmed; wear goggles and gloves. Please review and follow the safety guidelines at the beginning of this volume.

Procedure

1. Remove your fetal pig from the container of preservative. Gently rinse the pig under running water then pat dry with paper towels.

2. Place two layers of paper towels in the dissection tray. Lay the pig on the paper towels in a dissection tray.

3. A fetal pig has not been born. To determine its period of gestation, measure the pig's length (using a metric ruler) from the tip of its nose to the base of its tail. Use Data Table 1 to find out the pig's gestation period.

Data Table 1	
Length	**Days of gestation**
11 millimeters (mm)	21
17 mm	35
2.8 centimeters (cm)	49
4 cm	56
22 cm	100
30 cm	birth

4. Open the pig's mouth and gently run your finger over the gums. Describe what you feel in your science notebook.

5. Tear off 20 small pieces of masking tape, each piece about 1 inch (in.) (5 cm) long. Number the pieces of tape 1 through 20. Wrap each piece of tape around the top of a dissection pin.

6. Use Figures 2 and 3 (pages 11 and 12) as guides to help you locate and pin the structures listed on Data Table 2 (pages 12 and 13). Figure 2 labels some of the external anatomy of the pig. Figure 3 names the regions of the human body, many of which are similar to the regions of the pig's body.

7. Once you have inserted all of the pins, raise your hand and ask your teacher to check your work. If your pins are correctly positioned, the teacher will write a check mark on Data Table 2. If one or more pins are not in the correct position, your teacher will have you repeat step 6.

Analysis

1. Is your pig male or female? How do you know?
2. Describe the color(s) of the pig's skin.
3. Does the pig have any teeth? If so, how many?
4. Does the pig have eyelashes?
5. What is the common name for *nares*?

6. How many mammary papillae do male pigs have? How many do female pigs have?

7. Refer to Figure 3 to locate the following regions of the human body: anterior, posterior, dorsal, and ventral. On the pig, the head region is described as anterior and the tail region posterior. The term dorsal is used to describe the back and ventral the front, or belly side. In which region is each of these structures located? a: mouth; b: backbone; c: anus; d. mammary gland; e: chest.

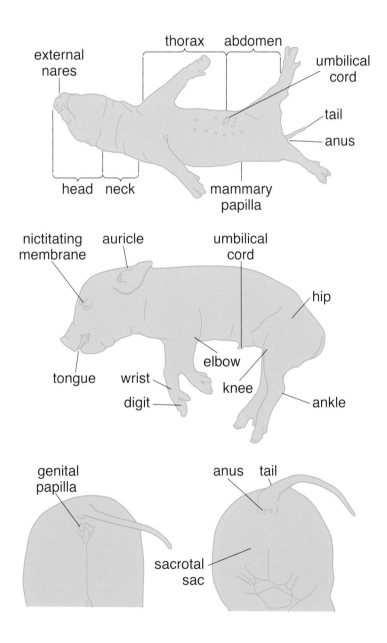

Figure 2

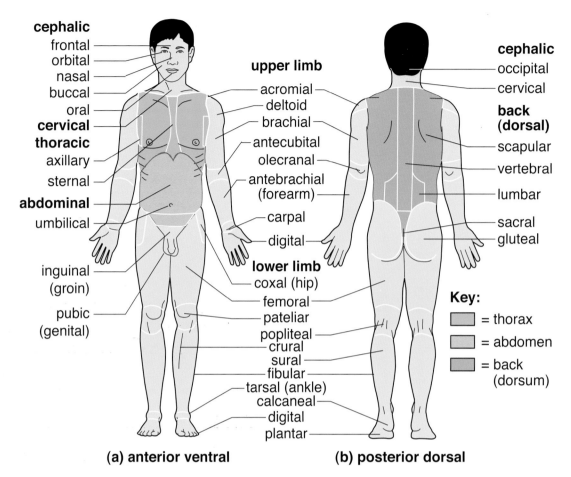

cephalic
- frontal
- orbital
- nasal
- buccal
- oral

cervical

thoracic
- axillary
- sternal

abdominal
- umbilical

- inguinal (groin)
- pubic (genital)

upper limb
- acromial
- deltoid
- brachial
- antecubital
- olecranal
- antebrachial (forearm)
- carpal
- digital

lower limb
- coxal (hip)
- femoral
- patellar
- popliteal
- crural
- sural
- fibular
- tarsal (ankle)
- calcaneal
- digital
- plantar

cephalic
- occipital
- cervical

back (dorsal)
- scapular
- vertebral
- lumbar
- sacral
- gluteal

Key:
- ▨ = thorax
- ▧ = abdomen
- ▩ = back (dorsum)

(a) anterior ventral   **(b) posterior dorsal**

Figure 3

Regions of the body

Data Table 2		
Body Structures	**Pin**	**Teacher approval**
Dorsal surface	1	
Ventral surface	2	
Anterior end	3	
Posterior end	4	
Lips	5	
External nares	6	
Auricle	7	

Data Table 2 (continued)		
Body Structures	**Pin**	**Teacher approval**
Nictitating membrane	8	
Tongue	9	
Papillae on tongue	10	
Mammary papillae	11	
Umbilical cord	12	
Penis (male only)	13	
Scrotal sac (male only)	14	
Genital papilla (female only)	15	
Body Regions		
Acromial area	16	
Patellar area	17	
Tarsal area	18	
Carpal area	19	
Olecranal area	20	

What's Going On?

Pigs and people have a lot of structures in common and some interesting differences. A pig has a *nictitating membrane* on each eye. Sometimes called a "third eyelid," this membrane is tough and semitransparent. It moves across the eye laterally instead of coming from the top or bottom of the eye like other eyelids. In many animals, like the shark, the nictitating membrane covers the eye during dangerous encounters, such as fights or feeding. In pigs, the membrane probably does not have any function, but it may have been useful in pigs' ancestors. Structures like the nictitating membrane that are no longer useful are known as *vestigial structures*.

The teeth of pigs are similar to those in humans. Both these mammals are *omnivores*, animals that eat plants and animals, so they have teeth for biting, teeth for tearing, and teeth for grinding. In the fetal pig, only a few tearing teeth, the canines, have erupted through the gums. In humans, the first teeth erupt about age 8 months.

The feet of pigs and people are significantly different. Pigs are ungulates, animals that walk on hooves. The first digits of the front and back hooves, which correspond to the human thumbs, are missing. The second and fifth digits are small, but functional. Hooves are derived from epithelial tissue, like fingernails.

Pigs have more mammary papillae, or nipples, than humans. Humans have two, whereas pigs have five to seven pairs. Multiple nipples are common in animals that have litters of offspring. A sow generally has eight to 12 babies in each litter. Like humans, nipples are found in males and females, but are only functional in adult females.

Connections

Fetal pigs are a by-product of the meat industry. They are not raised for dissection purposes. Once the sows are slaughtered, the unborn pigs are removed and preserved in a *formalin*, a chemical similar to embalming fluid. The fetal pig may be injected with colored latex. If so, an incision is made in the side of the neck. The arteries are filled with red latex and the veins with blue latex.

 ## Want to Know More?

See appendix for Our Findings.

Further Reading

"Fetal Pig Dissection," 2009 Teacher Tube. Available online. URL: http://www.teachertube.com/viewVideo.php?video_id=123355. Accessed October 4, 2009. Teacher Tube is a Web site of instructional videos for students or other teachers. On this site, a student examines and dissects a fetal pig while a teacher narrates.

Fleck, Earl W., Miso Mitkovski, and Mike Horn. "VPD, Virtual Fetal Pig Dissection," Whitman College and Walla Walla, Washington. Available online. URL: http://www.whitman.edu/biology/vpd/. Accessed October 4, 2009. This Web page gives students an alternative to dissection or a supplemental source of information during dissection.

Liang, Barbara. "Anatomical Terminology: Body Regions." Advanced Anatomy and Physiology. Wisc-Online. Available online. URL: http://www. wisc-online.com/objects/viewobject.aspx?ID=AP15405. Accessed March 21, 2010. This interactive tutorial lets students practice identifying body regions by their correct anatomical names.

ZeroBio. Fetal Pig Dissection Tutorial. Available online. URL: http://www. zerobio.com/videos/fetal_pig2.html. Accessed October 8, 2009. This Web site provides excellent photos and narration of fetal pig dissection.

3. Bone and Cartilage Structure

Topic

Bone and cartilage can be observed by dissecting a chicken wing.

Introduction

The body's skeletal system is primarily made up of two components: bone and cartilage. Bone is composed of *osseous cells* that are supported by a nonliving *matrix* of hard calcium salts. Bone tissue occurs in two types, compact and spongy. Compact bone is smooth and dense, whereas spongy bone contains a lot of open space. Bones are classified by their shapes as long, short, flat, or irregular.

The structure of a long bone is shown in Figure 1. The *periosteum* is a layer of protective connective tissue that covers the bone. The sides of the hollow shaft are made of compact bone, while the ends are spongy bone. The spaces in the spongy bone contain red marrow, which produces blood cells. The interior of a long bone has a *medullary cavity* that is lined with an *endosteum*. The medullary cavity contains yellow, fatty tissue.

Covering each end of the bone is a layer of *hyaline cartilage*. Cartilage is also found in places that need flexible support. The matrix of cartilage contains a lot of water, giving the tissue elasticity that is not found in bone. Hyaline cartilage, which has a shiny, blue-white appearance, is the most common type, occurring at the ends of bones. *Fibrocartilage* can be found between vertebrae, and *elastic cartilage* makes up the external ears. In this experiment, you will look at the bones and cartilage in a chicken wing and microscopically examine different types of cartilage.

Time Required

55 minutes

Materials

- ➥ raw chicken wing
- ➥ dissection tray

- scissors
- scalpel
- forceps
- dissecting microscope
- compound light microscope
- beaker (200 to 400 milliliters [ml])
- hot plate
- hot mitts
- access to water
- prepared slide of bone
- prepared slide of hyaline cartilage
- prepared slide of fibrocartilage
- prepared slide of elastic cartilage
- half Petri dish
- paper towels
- science notebook

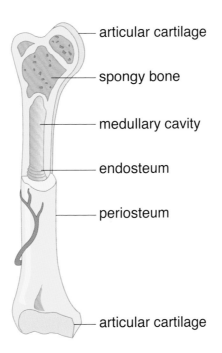

Figure 1

Structure of a long bone

Safety Note After the experiment, clean your desk with disinfectant and wash your hands and instruments with soap and hot water. Take care when working with the scalpel and the hot plate. Use hot mitts. Please review and follow the safety guidelines at the beginning of this volume.

Procedure, Part A

1. Answer Analysis questions 1 and 2.

2. Place a chicken wing on the dissection tray.

3. Using the scissors and scalpel, remove the skin and as much of the muscle as possible from the bones of the chicken wing. Leave the joint and cartilage intact.

4. Place the chicken wing in half a Petri dish and position it on the dissecting microscope. Locate the cartilage at the joint and observe it on medium and high powers. Sketch your observations in your science notebook. Answer Analysis question 3.

5. Put the chicken wing back in the dissection tray. Use the scalpel to separate the bones at the joints.

6. Wrap both ends of the longest bone in paper towels, then break the bone in half. Observe the interior of the broken bone and answer Analysis question 4.

7. Half fill a beaker with water. Place the unbroken long bones in the water. Place the beaker on the hot plate and and boil for 10 minutes.

8. Using the forceps, carefully remove the bones from the water and place them on a paper towel. Dry the bones and examine their external appearance. Answer Analysis question 5.

9. Wrap both ends of one of the boiled bones with paper towels. Break the bone in half and observe the interior. Answer Analysis question 6.

Procedure, Part B

1. Observe the prepared slide of compact bone under the compound light microscope. Sketch what you see in your science notebook.

2. Use the diagram in Figure 2 to help you label a central canal, lamella, and lacuna in your sketch.

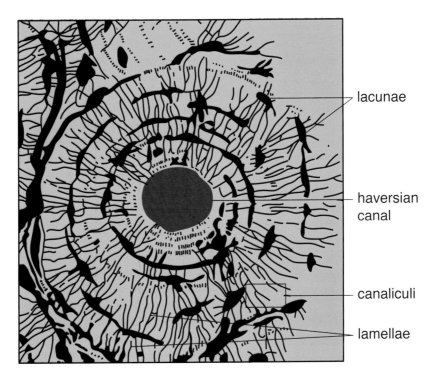

lacunae

haversian
canal

canaliculi

lamellae

Figure 2

Cross section of compact bone. The ring-shaped units are osteons.

3. Observe the prepared slide of hyaline cartilage under the compound light microscope. Sketch what you see in your science notebook. Label a lacuna, one of the spaces that holds a cell.

4. Observe the prepared slide of fibrocartilage under the compound light microscope. Sketch what you see in your science notebook. Label a lacuna.

5. Observe the prepared slide of elastic cartilage under the compound light microscope. Sketch what you see in your science notebook. Label a lacuna.

6. Answer Analysis question 7.

Analysis

1. What is the difference between spongy and compact bone tissue?
2. Where is cartilage found?
3. Describe the appearance of the cartilage at the joints.
4. Describe the following parts of the long bone you examined:
   a. endosteum   c. compact bone
   b. marrow   d. periosteum

5. How did the endosteum, marrow, compact bone, and periosteum look after boiling?

6. Which is easier to break: the raw bone or the boiled bone? Explain why.

7. How do the three types of cartilage differ?

What's Going On?

Microscopic examination of compact bone shows that it has a regular structure. Repeating, ring-shaped units called *osteons* give bone its strength (refer to Figure 2). Each osteon is made up of layers of matrix around a central canal. Central canals are connected to each other by smaller, volkmann's canals, which contain blood vessels and nerves. The layers of matrix, the lamellae, are dotted with spaces, the lacunae, where bone cells live. Lacunae are connected to each other by narrow canals, the *canaliculi*. Each central canal, its lamellae, lacunae, bone cells, and canaliculi, create a long cylinder known as a *haversian system*.

Hyaline cartilage, found at the ends of bones, is semitransparent and shiny. This type of cartilage is very strong and flexible. Much of the matrix is filled with strong collagen fibers. The *chondrocytes* or cartilage cells live in widely space lacunae. Besides the ends of bone, hyaline cartilage is also found in the larynx, trachea, tip of nose, and the connections between ribs and the breastbone. Hyaline cartilage reduces frictions at joints and helps hold bones together.

Fibrocartilage is very tough tissue that can be found between the discs of the spine, between the bones in the front of the pelvic girdle, and at the edges of some cavities where bones come together, such as the shoulder joint. In the spine, fibrocartilage absorbs shock. In joints, this tissue deepens the joint and therefore helps prevent dislocation.

Elastic cartilage is structurally similar to hyaline, but contains more elastic fibers. These fibers run through the cartilage matrix in all directions, giving structures flexibility while helping maintain their shape. The earlobe, epiglottis, and part of the larynx contain elastic cartilage.

Connections

Bones have bumps, ridges, and dips on them where muscles and tendons attach. Bone markings are classified into two categories, projections and depressions. A large, blunt projection is a trochanter, such as the greater and lesser trochanters on the femur (see Figure 3). A round projection is described as a tuberosity like the deltoid tuberosity of the humerus.

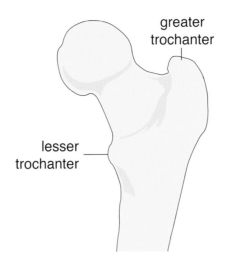

Figure 3

The femur shows some distinct processes.

The skull contains several interesting markings. The large, round opening in the base, the *foramen*, is a passageway for the spinal cord. A smaller hole, a *meatus*, accommodates a blood vessel or nerve. In the front of the skull are some open spaces called sinuses. These are filled with air and lined with moist, mucus membranes.

Want to Know More?

See appendix for Our Findings.

Further Reading

"Histology of Bone and Cartilage," Histology. Faculty of Medicine, University of Ottawa. Available online. URL: http://www.courseweb.uottawa.ca/medicine-histology/English/Musculoskeletal/default.htm#Cartilage. Accessed October 11, 2009. This extensive Web site provides excellent images of cartilage and bone and detailed descriptions of the tissues.

Johnson, D. R. "Introductory Anatomy: Bones." Centre for Human Biology, University of Leeds. Available online. URL: http://www.leeds.ac.uk/chb/lectures/anatomy3.html. Accessed October 11, 2009. Johnson gives an excellent overview of bone structure and function.

Trafton, Anne. "New Tissue Scaffold Regrows Cartilage and Bone," May 11, 2009. Physorg. Available online. URL: http://www.physorg.com/news161257258.html. Accessed October 11, 2009. Trafton explains the uses of a scaffold that medical practitioners can implant into damaged knees and other joints to speed healing of bone and cartilage.

4. Model of the Heart

Topic

Student-designed models can be used to explain the structures of the heart.

Introduction

Unless you experience a scare, it is unlikely that you notice your heart beating. Amazingly, the heart beats about 70 times a minute, 24 hours a day, 7 days a week. As it beats, the heart pumps blood through the body, sending oxygen, nutrients, and hormones to cells and removing wastes and carbon dioxide.

Located behind the protective sternum, the fist-sized heart weighs about 1 pound (lb) (2.2 kilograms [kg]). The organ works as two pumps that are separated from each other by a *septum*. Each pumping structure is made of a receiving chamber, an *atrium*, and a discharging chamber, a *ventricle* (see Figure 1). Oxygen-poor blood from the body enters the right atrium through two large veins, the *superior* and *inferior venae cavae*. From the right atrium, this blood flows into the right ventricle. When the right ventricle contracts, it pushes blood into a large vessel, the *pulmonary trunk*, which branches into the right and left *pulmonary arteries*. Each artery carries blood to one of the lungs. Oxygen-rich blood from the lungs travels back to the heart through four *pulmonary veins*. This blood flows into the left atrium, then enters the left ventricle. When the ventricle contracts, it pushes blood through the *aorta* to tissues all over the body. In this experiment, you will design and create a model that shows the chambers and vessels of the heart.

 Time Required

two 55-minute periods

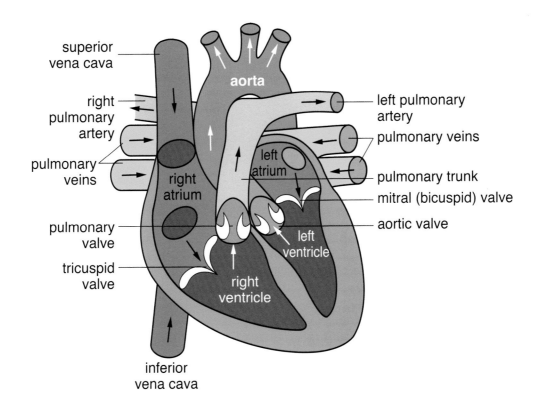

superior
vena cava

aorta

right
pulmonary
artery

pulmonary
veins

right
atrium

left pulmonary
artery

pulmonary veins

left
atrium

pulmonary trunk

mitral (bicuspid) valve

aortic valve

pulmonary
valve

left
ventricle

tricuspid
valve

right
ventricle

inferior
vena cava

Figure 1

Vessels and chambers of the heart

Materials

- access to a human anatomy and physiology text or the Internet
- cardboard
- stapler
- tape
- glue
- construction paper
- paper cups
- straws
- pipe cleaners
- science notebook

> **Safety Note**   Please review and follow the safety guidelines at the beginning of this volume.

Procedure

1. In anatomy books or on the Internet, research the structure and function of the human heart.

2. Answer Analysis questions 1 through 7.

3. Demonstrate the structures of the heart by designing and creating a model. Keep these points in mind when designing the model.

    a. Your model must show the following structures:
        - ✔ the four heart chambers
        - ✔ aorta
        - ✔ pulmonary trunk
        - ✔ left and right pulmonary arteries
        - ✔ four pulmonary veins
        - ✔ superior vena cava
        - ✔ inferior vena cava

    b. Each structure must be labeled with its name and an arrow showing direction of blood flow.

    c. You can use any of the materials provided by your teacher, but you do not need to use all of it.

    d. Once your model is constructed, you must be able to explain it to your teacher.

    e. Your grade will be assessed with the Heart Model Grading Rubric shown on page 27. Notice that the rubric addresses the required structures, the labels, neatness, and the Analysis questions.

4. Answer Analysis questions 8 through 15.

Analysis

1. What is the function of the atria? the ventricles?

2. Name and describe the valve between the right atrium and ventricle.

3. Name and describe the valve between the left atrium and ventricle.

4. Where is the pulmonary semilunar valve? What is its function?

5. Where is the aortic semilunar valve? What is its function?

6. Describe the path that blood follows through the body after it leaves the lungs.

7. What is the coronary circulation?

8. What is the destination of blood entering the pulmonary arteries? Where has this blood been?

9. Why are there two pulmonary arteries instead of one?

10. What is the destination of blood entering the pulmonary veins? Where has this blood been?

11. Why are there two pulmonary veins instead of one?

12. What is the source of blood in the superior vena cava?

13. What is the source of blood in the inferior vena cava?

14. How are the two atria similar?

15. How are the two ventricles similar?

What's Going On?

The heart has four chambers, two that receive blood and two that pump blood. The two chambers on the right side of the heart support the *pulmonary circulation*, collecting deoxygenated blood from the body and pumping it to the lungs (see Figure 2). Chambers on the left side of the heart serve as a *systemic* pump, taking oxygenated blood from the lungs and sending it to the body tissues. The two pumps are not exactly alike. The path of blood through the body is much longer than the circuit through the lungs. Therefore the left ventricle is larger and more muscular than the right.

Connections

The blood that is constantly traveling through the atria and ventricles does not nourish heart tissue. Instead, cardiac muscle tissue receives it own blood supply from a special group of vessels that make up the *coronary circulation*. Coronary arteries branch from the base of the aorta, fitting into the *coronary sulcus*, an indention on the heart's surface at the junction of the atria and ventricles (see Figure 3). When the ventricles are contracting, the coronary vessels are compressed, but during ventricular

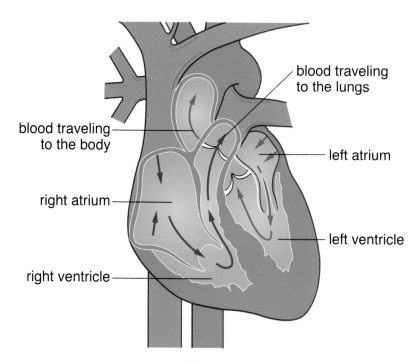

Figure 2

The flow of blood through the heart

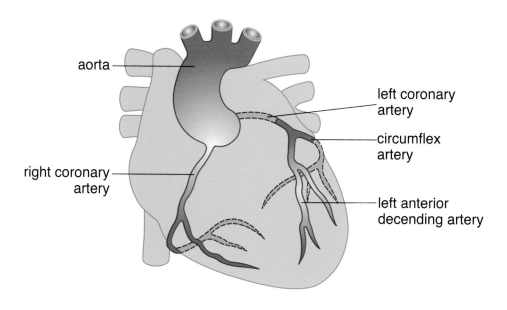

Figure 3

Vessels in the coronary circulation can be seen on the heart's surface

relaxation the vessels fill. Heart tissue is drained by several small cardiac veins that empty into a large vein at the back of the heart called the *coronary sinus.* This vein carries blood to the right atrium.

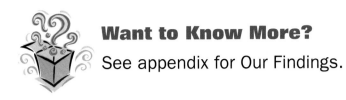

Want to Know More?

See appendix for Our Findings.

Heart Model Grading Rubric				
	Points Possible			
Requirements	**4**	**3**	**2**	**1**
Chambers	All four chambers are represented and labeled correctly.	All four chambers are represented but not all are labeled correctly.	Some, but not all, chambers are represented; some are labeled incorrectly.	Only one chamber is correctly represented and labeled.
Vessels	All seven vessels are represented and labeled correctly.	All seven vessels are represented but not all are labeled correctly.	Not all vessels are represented or labeled correctly.	Only one vessel is represented and labeled correctly.
Neatness	The model is neat and sturdy.	The model is neat but not sturdy.	The model is sturdy but not neat.	The model is neither neat nor sturdy.
Explanation	Explained all aspects of the heart and blood flow to the teacher.	Explained the chambers and some of the vessels.	Explained the chambers but none of the vessels.	Explained only one of the chambers and none of the vessels.
Analysis questions	Correctly answered thirteen or more Analysis questions.	Correctly answered nine or more Analysis questions.	Correctly answered five or more Analysis questions.	Correctly answered four or fewer Analysis questions.

Further Reading

Cable, Christopher. "The Auscultation Assistant," 2000. Available online. URL: http://www.wilkes.med.ucla.edu/inex.htm. Accessed October 13, 2009. The Auscultation Assistant, originally intended to help medical students improve their diagnostic skills, provides heart sounds.

Mayo Clinic. "Video: Heart and Circulatory System—How They Work," 2009. Available online. URL: http://www.mayoclinic.com/health/circulatory-system/MM00636. Accessed October 12, 2009. The staff at Mayo Clinic presents a video that explains how the heart works.

Virtual Cardiology Lab. HHMI Virtual Cardiology Lab. Available online. URL: http://www.hhmi.org/biointeractive/vlabs/cardiology/index.html. Accessed October 12, 2009. This virtual lab examines heritable diseases that affect the heart. Working as an intern, a user can examine a patient, use diagnostic tools, and develop a diagnosis.

5. Dissection of a Cow's Eye

Topic

Structures in a cow's eye are similar to those in a human's eye.

Introduction

The adult eye is a ball-shaped orb about 1 inch (in.) (2.5 centimeters [cm]) in diameter. Except for the anterior portion, the eye is enclosed in and protected by fat and bone. The outermost layer of the eyeball (see Figure 1) is covered with dense connective tissue that forms the *sclera*, or the white of the eye. Six muscles attached to the sclera of each eyeball give it a wide range of motion. In front of the pupil, the sclera is modified as a transparent *cornea*, which plays an important role is bending light rays. The cornea is covered by epithelium which joins the epithelial covering of the eyeball, the *conjunctiva*.

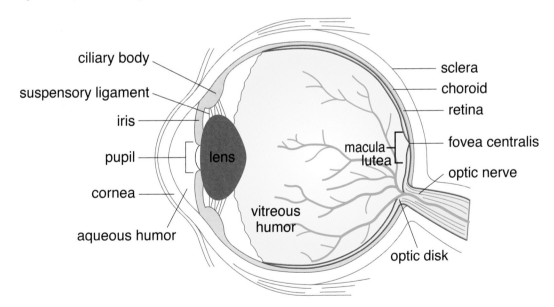

Figure 1

The middle layer of the eye, the *uvea*, contains vascular tissue. The three parts of the uvea are the *choroid,* the *ciliary body*, and the *iris*. The blood-rich choroid covers the back two-thirds of the eyeball. The brown color of the choroid, which is due to *melanocytes*, prevents light from reflecting inside the eyeball and causing visual confusion. Near the lens, the choroid is modified to form the *ciliary body*, a structure that holds the lens. The *iris*, the colored part of the eye, surrounds the lens and controls the amount of light entering its central opening, the *pupil*.

The eye's innermost layer, the sensory tunic, includes the *retina*. Retinal tissue is made up of light-sensitive receptor cells that convert light energy to electrical energy. All the processes of light-sensitive optic cells come together at the *optic disc*, the point where the optic nerve begins. The optic disc is a blind spot because there are no photoreceptor cells there. We are not aware of our blind spot because we have two eyes, and one compensates for the blind spot in the other.

The light-sensitive cells in the eyes are of two types: *rods* and *cones*. Rods operate well in dim light and are responsible for vision in black and white. Cones function only in bright light and provide us with color vision. Beside the blind spot on each retina is an oval region called the *macula lutea* that has a tiny pit in its center, the *fovea centralis*. This is a point of great visual acuity. The fovea in each eye is small, only about the size of the head of a pin.

The eye has two chambers. The small front chamber is between the cornea and lens. It is filled with *aqueous humor*, which is similar to blood plasma. The large back chamber is between the lens and the retina. It is filled with *vitreous humor*, a thicker fluid. Both fluids help nourish eye structures and give the eyeball its shape. In this experiment, you will dissect a cow's eyeball, examine the structures, and compare them to a human's eye.

Time Required
55 minutes

Materials
- preserved cow eye
- dissecting tray
- scalpel
- scissors
- gloves

- ✐ goggles
- ✐ forceps
- ✐ probe
- ✐ paper towels
- ✐ science notebook

Safety Note Take care when working with the preservative solution in which cow eye is embalmed. Wear goggles and gloves. Take care when working with a scalpel. Please review and follow the safety guidelines at the beginning of this volume.

Procedure

1. Answer Analysis question 1.

2. Remove the cow eye from the container. Rinse off any excess preserving fluid.

3. Place two or three paper towels in the dissecting tray. Lay the rinsed cow eye on the paper towels. Answer Analysis question 2.

4. Carefully remove the fat and the muscles from the exterior surface of the eyeball. As you work, avoid cutting the sclera or the optic nerve. The sclera connects to the cornea, which may be white or bluish-gray due to discoloration. The optic nerve is a small, stiff, cordlike structure that extends from the back of the eyeball.

5. Use the scalpel to cut a small hole in the cornea. Answer Analysis question 3.

6. Use the scalpel to slice the eye into a front half and a back half (see Figure 2). The front half will contain the cornea, lens, and iris. The back half will contain the retina and optic nerve.

7. After slicing the eye open, pour out the gel-like material that is found inside the orb. Answer Analysis question 4.

8. Lay the two cut halves of the eye on paper towels, cut sides up. Closely examine the front half of the eyeball. Use the probe to touch the lens gently, moving it slightly so that you can see how it is attached to the dark-colored ciliary body. Outside of the ciliary body is the iris, a muscle that controls the size of the pupil. Answer Analysis question 5.

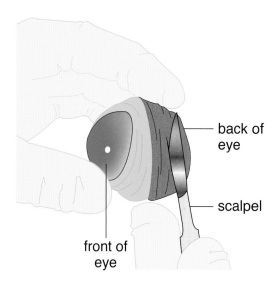

back of
eye

scalpel

front of
eye

Figure 2

To view the interior of the eye, cut the eye in half.

9. Turn the front half of the eye upside down. Remove the cornea from the eyeball. Look through the cornea. Notice that despite its discoloration, the cornea is still somewhat transparent.

10. Remove the lens from the eyeball. Hold the lens over some small print and try to read through it. Squeeze the lens gently to test its flexibility. Answer Analysis question 6.

11. On the back half of the eye, examine the white, tissue-thin material, the retina. Notice how the retina gathers at one point to form the optic disc. See if you can find the macula lutea and the tiny pit in its center, the fovea centralis.

12. Use forceps to gently remove the retina from the back of the eye. Below the retina is the choroid layer. In humans, this layer is very dark to absorb light that may interfere with vision. In cows and some other animals, the layer is reflective, which enables cows to see better at night than humans do. Answer Analysis question 7.

13. Once you can identify all of the structures listed on the data table, raise your hand and point them out to your teacher. When you identify a structure correctly, your teacher will put a check mark next to it on the data table.

Data Table	
Body structures	**Teacher approval**
Adipose tissue	
External muscle tissue	
Cornea	
Sclera	
Iris	
Ciliary body	
Lens	
Retina	
Choroid layer	
Optic nerve	

Analysis

1. What are the functions of the following structures:
    a. sclera
    b. cornea
    c. pupil
    d. iris
    e. choroid layer
    f. retina
    g. optic nerve
2. Describe the appearance of the cow's eye.
3. What is the fluid that drained out of the hole you cut in the cornea?
4. What is the gel-like material that fills most of the eye?

5. Describe the appearance of the iris.

6. What did you see when you looked at small print through the lens?

7. Describe the choroid layer in the cow's eye.

What's Going On?

Although the cow's eye is much larger than the eye of an adult human, many of the structures are the same. In both species, the lens is located in the front of the eye, directly behind the cornea and in front of the pupil. The jobs of the cornea and the lens are to bend light rays so that they focus on the retina. In life, the lens is flexible so it can change shape. The ciliary muscles can change the curvature of the lens. If an object is close, the ciliary muscles contract and make the lens thick, creating a rounder lens that causes light waves to bend a lot. To focus on an object that is far away, the ciliary muscles relax and let the lens flatten, causing light rays to bend only a little.

The bulk of the lens is made up of thin, tightly packed layers of cells called lens fibers. The cells are stretched from the anterior to the posterior end of the lens. When the lens is cut in cross section, the arrangement of the fibers creates layers. The individual cells are held together by interlocking extensions and by *gap junctions*, special intercellular connections.

Connections

The human body is equipped with several types of cells that can pick up stimuli from the external environment. Some of the cells, like those that detect touch, are considered general receptors. The special senses are those that are equipped with unique sensory cells. These senses, which include vision, hearing, smell, and equilibrium, are located in the head within distinct organs or tissues. In humans, vision is the predominant sense. More than 70 percent of a human's sensory receptors are dedicated to vision.

 ## Want to Know More?

See appendix for Our Findings.

Further Reading

"Activity: The Structure of the Eye." Available online. URL: http://www. sumanasinc.com/webcontent/toolsamples/sampledd.html. Accessed October 15, 2009. This Shockwave activity lets you match terms and definitions to eye structures.

"Eye Diseases," October 8, 2009. Medline Plus. Available online. URL: http://www.nlm.nih.gov/medlineplus/eyediseases.html. Accessed October 15, 2009. Supported by the National Institutes of Health, this Web site provides links to dozens of sources that discuss eye diseases.

Kolb, Helga, Eduardo Fernandez, and Ralph Nelson. "Webvision; the Organization of the Retina and Visual System," August 2009. John Moran Eye Center, University of Utah. Available online. URL: http://webvision. med.utah.edu/index.html. Accessed October 14, 2009. This Web site provides an excellent description of eye structures and explains how they work.

6. Food Analysis

Topic

Foods vary in the types of nutrients they contain.

Introduction

You may have heard the expression, "You are what you eat." This expression is true to some extent. Some of the food we eat is used to build the molecules that make up our body. However, most of it is converted to *ATP, adenosine triphosphate*, the high-energy molecule that runs chemical reactions (see Figure 1). The energy value of food is measured in kilocalories (kcal), also known as "large" calories (C). A kilocalorie is the amount of heat needed to raise the temperature of one kilogram of water 1 degree Celsius (°C) (33.8 degrees Fahrenheit [°F]).

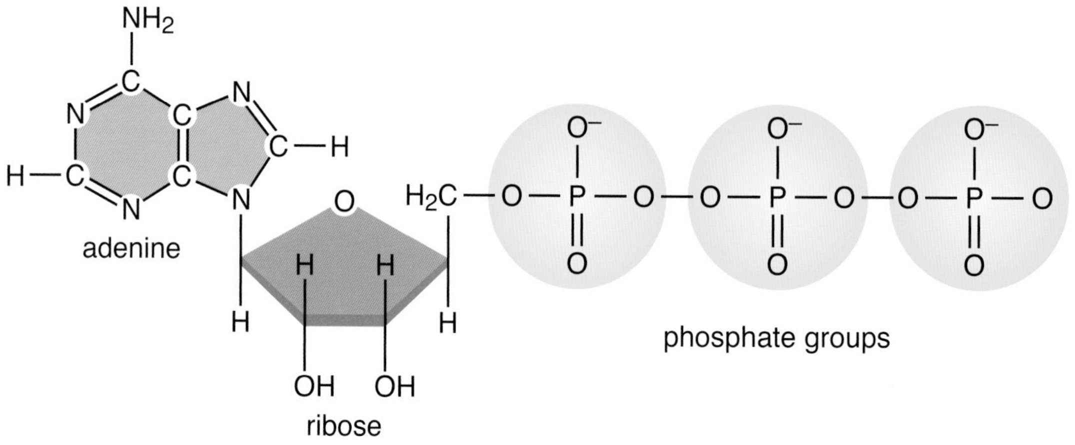

Figure 1

A molecule of ATP is made up of the nitrogen base adenine, the sugar ribose, and three phosphate groups.

In the digestive system, foods are broken down mechanically and chemically so the *nutrients*, chemicals that the body can use for growth and maintenance, can be absorbed by the body. Not all foods provide us with the same nutrients. The major nutrients are carbohydrates, lipids, and proteins. The minor nutrients, those needed in smaller quantities, are minerals and vitamins. Water is not classified as a nutrient, although it is essential in dissolving nutrients and providing a medium in which biochemical reactions can take place. In this experiment, you will be given 10 food samples. You will set up an experiment to test each sample for the presence of lipids, complex carbohydrates, simple carbohydrates, and protein.

Time Required

55 minutes

Materials

- 10 food samples
- scalpel
- stirring rod
- 2 test tubes
- test-tube rack
- test-tube holder
- hot mitts or oven mitts
- 2 beakers, 200 to 400 milliliter [ml]
- 10 ml graduated cylinder
- hot plate
- pipette or dropper
- iodine solution in dropper bottle
- biuret solution
- Benedict's solution
- brown paper
- scissors
- distilled water
- access to water
- pepsin
- IM hydrochloric acid (a few drops)

Safety Note   Take care when working with the hot plate and hot water. Use hot mitts. Be careful with the scalpel and when using acid. Please review and follow the safety guidelines at the beginning of this volume.

Procedure

1. Answer Analysis questions 1 through 3.

2. Design a data table on which you can list the food items to be tested and indicate whether or not the foods contain lipids, complex carbohydrates, simple carbohydrates, or proteins.

3. Develop and write procedures for testing each food sample for the presence of lipids, complex carbohydrates, simple carbohydrates, or proteins. You can use any of the supplies provided by your teacher, but you may not need to use all of them. The tests you need to perform are described below. Once you have read the directions for each test and written a procedure for this experiment, show your procedures to your teacher. If you get teacher approval, carry out the tests and record the results. If not, modify your work and show it to your teacher again.

   a. *Lipid Test.* To test a food for the presence of lipids, gently rub a sample on a piece of brown paper. Set the paper aside until it dries. Hold the dried paper up to the light to see if a grease spot is present. A grease spot indicates the presence of lipids.

   b. *Complex Carbohydrate Test.* Place one drop of iodine onto a food sample. If the iodine turns blue or black, starch is present. Starch is a complex carbohydrate. If the iodine remains red or brown, starch is not present. To clarify an ambiguous test result, put a little of the food sample in a small test tube half filled with distilled water. Stir the sample to mix well. Add a few drops of iodine and check the color.

   c. *Simple Carbohydrate Test.* Prepare a boiling water bath by putting a beaker half filled with water on a hot plate. Heat the beaker until it reaches a gentle boil. Stir a small sample of food to be tested into a test tube half filled with distilled water. Make sure that the food and water are mixed well. Add 1 ml Benedict's solution to the test tube. Place the test tube in the hot water bath for 1 minute (see Figure 2). Examine the color of the contents of the test tube. If the contents are orange, simple

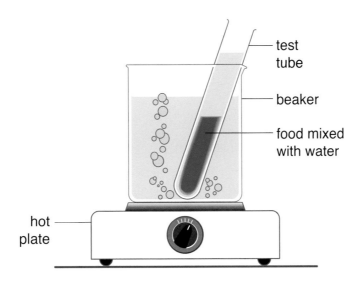

Figure 2

Boiling water bath

carbohydrates like glucose are present. If the contents remain blue, simple carbohydrates are not present.

  d. *Protein Test.* Stir a small sample of food to be tested into a test tube half filled with distilled water. Make sure that the food and water are mixed well. Add 5 drops of biuret solution to the test tube. Set aside the test tube for 1 minute. A positive test for protein is a change in color from blue to pink or violet. To clarify an ambiguous test result, prepare another test tube of food mixed with distilled water. Add 1 ml of pepsin and 1 ml of hydrochloric acid to the test tube. Gently mix. Set aside the test tube for 5 minutes. Add 5 drops of biuret solution. Set aside the test tube for 1 minute. Compare the color to your earlier findings.

  4. Follow your teacher's instructions for disposing of the food samples and the materials in the test tubes.

  5. Answer Analysis questions 4 through 8.

Analysis

  1. What are the major nutrients found in food?

  2. How can an individual be sure of getting all of the major nutrients each day?

  3. Why are the minor nutrients described as "minor"?

4. Which foods used in the experiment contain more than one of the basic nutrients?

5. Which is the source of most of the carbohydrates in our diets, plants or animals?

6. Name three foods that provide lipids.

7. Name five foods that provide protein.

8. Why do you think the digestive system breaks up food and mixes it with enzymes and hydrochloric acid?

What's Going On?

Most of our food is made up of carbohydrates, lipids, and proteins. These three major nutrients are available in varying amounts in different foods. For example, corn contains corn starch and corn oil and milk contains milk sugar (lactose), protein, and fat. Prepared dishes, like pizza, are made up of several kinds of foods, each of which may contain more than one type of major nutrient.

Carbohydrates are primarily derived from plant sources. In the body, complex carbohydrates are converted to simple forms such as glucose, the primary carbohydrate molecule used by cells. Glucose is converted to ATP, so it is essential for our survival. Lipids are consumed as neutral fats or *triglycerides*, each molecule of which contains glycerol and three fatty acids.

Lipids in our diet may be *saturated* or *unsaturated*. Saturated fats are found in animal-derived foods and a few plants, such as coconut. Seeds, nuts, grains, and other vegetable oils are unsaturated. In the diet, fats help the body absorb lipid-soluble vitamins and provide energy to muscle cells. Fats are also used to make the *myelin sheath* around neurons and the plasma membranes of all cells.

Proteins are classified by the essential amino acids they contain. A complete protein is one that contains all essential amino acids needed for growth. Animal-derived proteins fall into this category. Incomplete proteins lack one or more of the essential amino acids. For example, leafy green vegetables lack one essential amino acid and beans lack a different amino acid. Vegetarians must plan their diets so that they take in all the amino acids needed to build proteins.

Connections

The digestive system is in charge of taking in food, breaking it down into usable molecules, absorbing those molecules, and getting rid of unwanted wastes. Organs of the digestive system (shown in Figure 3) fall into two categories: the *alimentary canal* and the accessory organs. The alimentary canal is a long, muscular tube that begins with the mouth and includes the *pharynx*, esophagus, stomach, small intestine, and large intestine. These organs grind, churn, and mix food with chemicals, absorb useful molecules, and collect wastes.

Accessory organs are the teeth, tongue, gallbladder, liver, and pancreas. The teeth and tongue are important in the mixing and mechanical breakdown of food, and salivary glands in the mouth contribute secretions that begin chemical digestion. Other organs and glands add the chemicals needed to complete the breakdown of food.

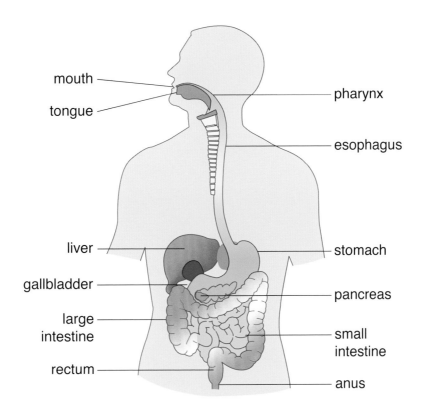

Figure 3

Organs of digestive system

Want to Know More?

See appendix for Our Findings.

Further Reading

Bowen, R. A., Laura Austgen, and Melissa Rouge. "Pathophysiology of the Digestive System," July 5, 2006. Available online. URL: http://www.vivo.colostate.edu/hbooks/pathphys/digestion/index.html. Accessed October 18, 2009. This hypertext prepared by veterinarians at the University of Colorado contains core, advanced, and supplemental material on the digestive system.

"The Digestive System," 2009. Inner Body. Available online. URL: http://www.innerbody.com/image/digeov.html. Accessed October 18, 2009. This interactive Web site lets you click on a body structure, see its location, and read a description of its function.

"Your Digestive System and How It Works," April 2008. National Institutes of Health. Available online. URL: http://digestive.niddk.nih.gov/ddiseases/pubs/yrdd/. Accessed October 18, 2009. This Web site provides information about the structures and functions of the digestive system as well as the nutrients in food.

7. Urinalysis

Topic

Analysis of urine samples can provide information about a person's health.

Introduction

The kidneys are relatively small organs located in the dorsal region of the abdomen. The job of the kidneys is to regulate the volume and composition of body fluids. To carry out this job, the kidneys filter blood and reabsorb important molecules. Despite their size, these two organs handle a large volume of blood. Each time the heart beats, 25 percent of the blood leaving the heart travels to the kidneys. Urine formed in the kidneys flow through *ureters* to the *bladder*, where it is stored temporarily (see Figure 1).

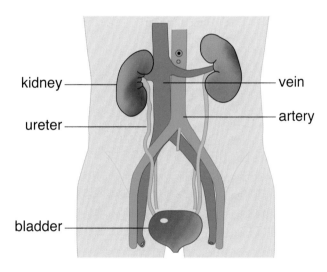

Figure 1

Blood flows into the kidneys at a high rate of speed. Molecules and water in the blood are forced out as the material is filtered through coils of small vessels. Essential molecules such as sugars and amino acids are reabsorbed and retained by the body. Unwanted molecules and unneeded water are left in the filtrate and become part of the urine.

The makeup of urine can provide information about one's health. Some diseases can be diagnosed by the presence or absence of certain molecules in the urine. For example, glucose is usually reabsorbed, so is not normally present in urine. Data Table 1 provides some information that can be gained through tests on urine. In this experiment, you will use a patient's medical history and carry out some tests on his or her "urine" to make a diagnosis.

Data Table 1	
Abnormal finding in urine	**Notes and indications**
Low volume of urine	Normal level: 2 liters/day (L/d) (2.11 quarts/day [qt/d]). Low volume may indicate dehydration or damage to kidneys.
High volume of urine	Normal level: 2 L/d (2.1 qt/d). High volume may indicate diabetes.
Low pH	Normal: near 7 Low PH may be due to large amount of meat in diet. May indicate diabetes or dehydration.
High pH	Normal: near 7 High PH may be due to little meat and a large amount of plant matter in diet. May indicate aspirin overdose or kidney disease.
Glucose	Normal: none (or minute amounts) present Glucose in the urine can indicate diabetes. Glucose in urine causes more water to be excreted, so diabetics lose a lot of water and are often very thirsty.
Ketones	Normal: none present Ketones in urine indicate starvation, some diseases, and diabetes. Ketones are the breakdown products of fat metabolism. They can be seen in dieters avoiding carbohydrates.
Proteins	Normal: none present Protein may indicate a disease in the kidneys or a bacterial infection. Kidney disease can result from many factors, including high blood pressure and autoimmune syndromes like lupus.

Data Table 1 (continued)	
Abnormal finding in urine	**Notes and indications**
Nitrite	Normal: none present Nitrite indicates bacterial infection. Bacteria change nitrate to nitrite. Individuals with a kidney infection may be unaware of the problem because they do not experience pain with urination. However, bacterial infection of the urethra or bladder does cause pain.
Blood	Normal: none present Blood cells indicate bleeding in the urinary system Some bacterial infections and kidney stones can cause bleeding.
Sediment or crystals	Normal: none present Sediment may indicate kidney stones. Stone-forming minerals are calcium and oxalate, which are found in green, leafy vegetables.
Chloride	Normal: present in small amounts Larger quantities may indicate vomiting. Loss of chloride into urine can cause muscle cramps.

Time Required

55 minutes

Materials

- access to human anatomy and physiology textbooks or Internet
- distilled water
- pH paper
- 6 pipettes or droppers
- 6-well well plate
- hot plate
- hot mitts or oven mitts
- beaker
- Benedict's solution

- biuret solution
- 6 test tubes
- test-tube rack
- test-tube clamp
- silver nitrate solution
- 6 simulated urine samples (labeled 1 through 6)
- science notebook

Procedure, Part A

1. Test the pH of urine sample 1. To do so:
   a. Tear off a small strip of pH paper.
   b. Collect a few drops of urine with a clean pipette.
   c. Drop the urine on the pH paper.
2. Compare the color of the pH paper to the color of the chart on the paper's dispenser.
3. Rinse the pipette with distilled water.
4. Record the pH on Data Table 2.
5. Repeat steps 1 through 4 with the other urine samples.

Procedure, Part B

1. Test the urine sample for chloride ions. To do so:
   a. Rinse the well plate with distilled water.
   b. Label the six wells in the well plate 1 through 6.
   c. Add 2 drops of urine sample 1 to well 1.
   d. Repeat step c for the five other samples.
   e. Add 1 drop of silver nitrate solution to each urine sample. Gently shake the well plate to mix.
   f. Observe any changes. A white precipitate indicates presence of chloride ion.

2. Record the presence or absence of chloride ion on Data Table 2.

Procedure, Part C

1. Set up a boiling water bath by putting a beaker half filled with water on a hot plate and heating the beaker until the water reaches a gentle boil.

2. Test the urine samples for the presence of glucose. To do so:

   a. Label six test tubes 1 through 6.

   b. Pour 1 milliliter (ml)(0.33 ounces [oz]) of urine sample 1 into test tube 1.

   c. Repeat step b for the other five samples.

   d. Add 1 ml (0.32 oz) of Benedict's solution to each test tube.

   e. Place all six test tubes in the hot water bath for 2 minutes (min).

   f. Remove the test tubes from the hot water bath and place in a test-tube rack.

   g. Observe any changes. A color change from blue to orange indicates the presence of glucose.

3. Record the presence or absence of glucose on Data Table 2.

Procedure, Part D

1. Test the urine samples for the presence of protein. To do so:

   a. Rinse the well plate with distilled water.

   b. Label the wells in the well plate 1 through 6.

   c. Add 2 drops of urine sample 1 to well 1.

   d. Repeat step c for the other samples.

   e. Add 2 drops of biuret solution to each urine sample. Gently shake the well plate to mix.

   f. Observe any changes. A change in color to violet indicates the presence of protein.

2. Record the presence or absence of protein on Data Table 2.

Procedure, Part E

1. Suppose urine samples 1 through 6 came from patients 1 through 6. Read each patient's medical history. Use the information in the history to complete the last two columns on Data Table 2.

- Patient 1. Female; 30 years old; interested in health food; vegetarian; blood in urine; crystals in urine; volume 0.6 L/d (0.63 qt/d).
- Patient 2. Male; 17 years old; feels unusually tired; no sediment; volume 3.3 L/d (3.5 qt/d)
- Patient 3. Female; 21 years old; rash on face; pain in joints; no sediment; volume 2.0 L/d (2.11 qt/d)
- Patient 4. Female; 19 years old; pain with urination; nitrites in urine; red and white blood cells in urine; 1.9 L/d (2 qt/d)
- Patient 5. Male; 16 years old; complains of cold or flu symptoms and vomiting; no sediment; volume 1.1 L/d (1.16 qt/d)
- Patient 6. Female; 18 years old; urinalysis for regular yearly check up; no sediment; volume 2.01 L/d (2.12 qt/d)

2. Using all of the information in the medical histories and from your lab tests, diagnose each patient. If you need more information, refer to your textbook or the Internet. Use your diagnoses to answer Analysis question 1.

3. Answer Analysis questions 2 through 6.

Data Table 2						
Urine Sample	pH	Chloride ion	Glucose	Protein	Volume (L/d)	Blood crystals or sediment
1						
2						
3						
4						
5						
6						

Analysis

1. Indicate your diagnosis for each patient:

   Patient 1 _____

   Patient 2 _____

   Patient 3 _____

   Patient 4 _____

   Patient 5 _____

   Patient 6 _____

2. Which patient's urine showed no abnormal findings?

3. Why is the urine volume of patient 2 so high?

4. What causes the crystalline sediment in the urine of patient 1?

5. Why might the body form a small amount of concentrated urine?

6. You have a new patient, an 18-year-old male who is trying out for the wrestling team. He normally weighs 200 pounds, but wants to wrestle at 180. He has ketones in his urine and a very small volume of urine.

   a. What is the source of the ketones?

   b. What advise can you give him?

What's Going On?

The cases presented in the experiment showed how urine tests can help detect some health problems. Urine is produced by a complex system of filtration and reabsorption in which unwanted substances are left in the urine so that they can be removed from the body. As a result, the kidneys can rid the body of high levels of unwanted materials very quickly while maintaining the desired composition of blood and other body fluids.

The functional unit of the kidney is the *nephron*. Within each nephron are hundreds of units of *glomerular* capillaries surrounding a *Bowman's capsule* (see Figure 2). The filtration barrier between the capillaries and capsule is not very selective, so the only things that are not filtered out of the blood at this point are blood cells and blood proteins. Water, minerals, hormones, fats, dissolved salt, and sugars are filtered. These substances leave the capsule and travel through the *renal tubule*, the place where valuable substances are reabsorbed. Salt and water are reabsorbed if they are needed. The waste products of metabolism and any materials that are potentially toxic are not reabsorbed and become part of the urine.

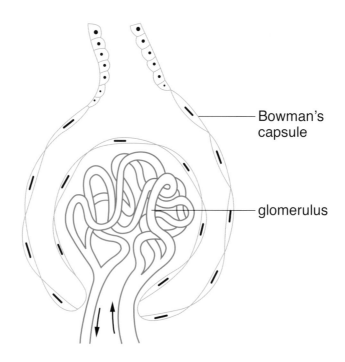

Figure 2
Nephron structure

Connections

Commercial test strips make it simple for medical practitioners to test urine. Some strips test for glucose only while others include tests for ketones, protein, pH, nitrites, blood, and specific gravity. Most urinalysis test strips are pieces of plastic to which chemically specific pads of chemicals are attached. The chemicals in the pads react with the sample of urine within 30 seconds (sec) to 1 min and change colors (see Figure 3). The colors are then compared to a color chart to find the level of each tested factor. The strips are disposable.

 Want to Know More?

See appendix for Our Findings.

Further Reading

Klatt, Edward C. "Urinalysis," 2009. Internet Pathology Laboratory for medical Education. Available online. URL: http://library.med.utah.edu/WebPath/TUTORIAL/URINE/URINE.html. Accessed October 25, 2009.

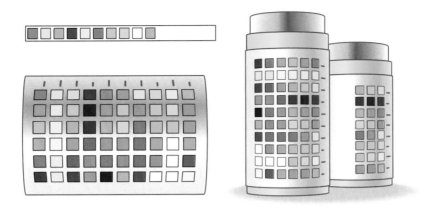

Figure 3

Pads of chemicals on test strips change colors when they react to substances in urine.

Klatt, of Mercer School of Medicine in Savannah, Georgia, provides information on a urinalysis as a resource for students and workers in health care.

Roxe, David M. "Urinalysis," 1990. Clinical Methods. Available online. URL: http://www.ncbi.nlm.nih.gov/bookshelf/br.fcgi?book=cm& part=A5417. Accessed October 25, 2009. Roxe explains the technique of urinalysis and gives some of the basic science behind the tests.

"Urinalysis Test," May 17, 2005. How Stuff Works. Available online. URL: http://healthguide.howstuffworks.com/urinalysis-dictionary.htm. Accessed October 25, 2009. This Web page explains the test and lists some of the conditions that urinalysis might indicate.

8. Osmosis in Red Blood Cells

Topic

Hypertonic, hypotonic, and isotonic solutions have different effects on red blood cells.

Introduction

Erythrocytes, or red blood cells, carry oxygen from the lungs to cells in all the body's tissues. Erythrocytes are small compared to other blood cells and have a biconcave shape (see Figure 1). These cells live in a watery environment, the straw-colored liquid called *plasma*. Even though water constantly moves across the *selectively permeable membranes* of cells, the amount of water within the cells remains relatively constant. This equilibrium is due to the fact that the amount of water moving into the cell is roughly equivalent to the amount moving out.

Figure 1

Normal red blood cells

If the concentration of solutes in blood plasma changes, erythrocytes may gain or lose water by *osmosis*, the movement of water across a membrane caused by differences in solute concentrations on the two sides of the membrane. In this laboratory, you will design an experiment to find out how solutions of various concentrations affect red blood cells.

 Time Required

55 minutes

Materials

- compound light microscope
- microscope slides
- cover slips
- well plate
- blood (from veterinarian or slaughter house)
- distilled water
- physiological saline (or 0.9 percent NaCl)
- salt water
- 3 pipettes or droppers
- hot plate
- hot mitts
- gloves
- science notebook

Safety Note Take care when working with the hot plate and hot water. Use hot mitts. Wear gloves when working with blood.
Please review and follow the safety guidelines at the beginning of this volume.

Procedure

1. Your job is to design and perform an experiment to find out the effects of three solutions on red blood cells: physiological saline (0.9 percent NaCl), distilled water, and salt water.

2. Answer Analysis questions 1 and 2.

3. Before you conduct your experiment, decide exactly what you are going to do. Write the steps you plan to take (your experimental procedure) and the materials you plan to use (materials list) on Data Table 1. You can use any of the supplies provided by your teacher, but you may not need to use all of them.

4. Show your procedure and materials list to the teacher. If you get teacher approval, proceed with your experiment. If not, modify your work and show it to your teacher again.

Data Table	
Your experimental procedure	
Your materials list	
Teacher's approval	

5. If you want to make a slide of blood cells as part of your experiment, keep in mind the general procedure for making a *blood smear*. This technique spreads the blood cells so that they are not piled up, obscuring each other when viewed under the microscope.

    a. Place a very small dot of blood near one end of the slide. (If you get too much blood on the slide, blot part of it with paper towels.)

    b. Position a cover slip, the spreader, so that it touches the drop. Angle the cover slip at 30 to 40 degrees (see Figure 2).

c. Push the spreader across the slide in a quick motion. The blood smear should cover about half the slide.

d. Put the cover slip on the smear. If the smear is large, you may need two covers slips. Examine the slides under the microscope to find a region where the cells are spread out and easy to view.

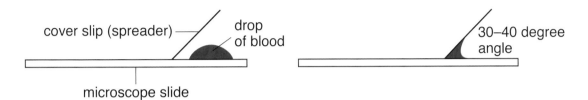

cover slip (spreader) — drop of blood

microscope slide

30–40 degree angle

Figure 2

How to make a blood smear

6. Once you have teacher approval, assemble the materials you need and begin your procedure.

7. Collect your results on a data table of your own design.

8. Answer Analysis questions 3 through 5.

Analysis

1. What effect do you think the following solutions will have on red blood cells: (a) distilled water; (b) salt water; (c) physiological saline.

2. Examine the diagram in Figure 3 to answer the following questions:

a. Would you expect the blue solute molecules to flow across the semipermeable membrane? If so, in what direction?

b. Would you expect the red water molecules to flow across the semipermeable membrane? If so, in what direction?

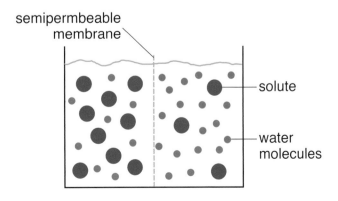

semipermbeable membrane

solute

water molecules

Figure 3

3. Describe the effects of the three solutions on red blood cells.

4. A solution of 0.9 percent salt is isotonic to blood cells. Seawater is about 2.5 percent salt. What will happen to blood cells in seawater? Why?

5. Complete Data Table 2.

Data Table 2			
	Concentration of solute in cells (low or high)	**Concentration of solute surrounding cells (low or high)**	**Direction in which water molecules move (into or out of cells)**
Hypotonic solution			
Hypertonic solution			
Isotonic solution			

What's Going On?

In your experiment, you exposed red blood cells to solutions containing varying amounts of salt, a solute. One way to mix the cells and the solution is by placing a little of the solution on a blood smear slide at the edge of the cover slip. Another way is to put some blood in well plates of different solutions. When discussing these solutions, three terms are important to know: *isotonic*, *hypertonic*, and *hypotonic*. An isotonic solution is one that has the same amount of solute as the cell. Plasma and physiological saline are isotonic. In this type of solution, red blood cells maintain their normal biconcave shapes (see Figure 4).

Distilled water contains no solutes, so it is hypotonic to the solutions in cells. Because the concentration of water is greater outside the cells than inside, water molecules diffuse into the cells, causing them to swell and become round. Rounded cells may burst, causing them to appear flattened or jagged along the edges.

Salt water contains more solutes than the solution inside of cells. Another way to say this is that the concentration of water molecules inside the cells is greater than outside the cells. As a result, water moved out of the cells which caused them to shrivel and appear spiky.

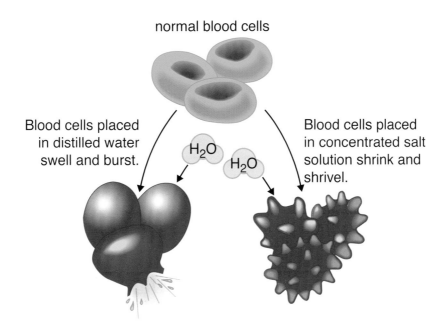

normal blood cells

Blood cells placed in distilled water swell and burst.

H_2O

H_2O

Blood cells placed in concentrated salt solution shrink and shrivel.

Figure 4

Connections

An understanding of the movement of water across a cell's membrane is critical to medical practitioners. Medications that are delivered intravenously are dissolved in isotonic solutions. If a patient receives intravenous medication in distilled water or in water that contains a large amount of solute, their blood cells could be destroyed. The destruction of red blood cells is a life-threatening condition called *hemolysis.*

During surgery, some patients opt to use a *cell-saver*, a device that collects the blood they lose during surgery so that it can be returned to their bodies. Cell-savers prevent the need for transfusions from donors. Part of the cell-saving procedure is to "wash" the scavenged blood cells with 0.9 percent saline. If the blood is washed with sterile water, the cells *lyse* and are useless to the patient.

Want to Know More?

See appendix for Our Findings.

Further Reading

Bell, K. N. I. "Osmosis Troubles a Lot of People, So for Those of You Who Are Still Confused . . .". Available online. URL: http://www.mun.ca/biology/Help_centre/1001_2_tutorialpages/OSMOSIS.html. Accessed October 21, 2009. Dr. Bell's tutorial on osmosis explains the basic principles of water movement across cell membranes.

Brown, Terry. "Osmosis," 1999. Available online. URL: http://www.tvdsb.on.ca/WESTMIN/science/sbi3a1/cells/Osmosis.htm. Accessed October 24, 2009. This interactive Web page shows how molecules of water behave in solutions of different concentrations.

Farabee, M. J. "Transport In and Out of Cells," *Online Biology Book,* June 6, 2007. Available online. URL: http://www.emc.maricopa.edu/faculty/farabee/BIOBK/BioBooktransp.html. Accessed October 21, 2009. Farabee's *Online Biology Book* provides information on all topics of biological science. This chapter covers all aspects of osmosis through cell membranes.

9. Types of Muscles

Topic

The structures of different types of muscles vary along with their functions.

Introduction

You have three different types of muscles in your body: skeletal muscles, cardiac muscles, and smooth muscles. Each muscle type has unique functions and characteristics that distinguish it from the other types of muscles (see Figure 1).

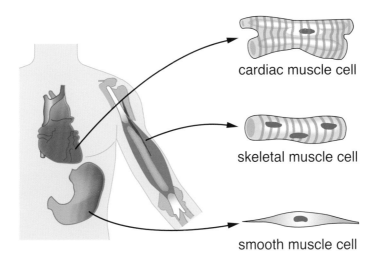

cardiac muscle cell

skeletal muscle cell

smooth muscle cell

Figure 1

Skeletal muscles are attached to the bony skeleton and are the primary "machines" for body movement. Skeletal muscles are made of long, thin cells called *muscle fibers* that appear banded when you look at them under a microscope. The bands, called *striations,* are created by the arrangement of proteins in the cells. Muscle fibers are unique in that they are *multinucleate,* having many nuclei in each cell. Skeletal muscles are also *voluntary*, meaning you have control over them and you can move them when you want. Skeletal muscles can be very strong, but they tire or fatigue easily. They cannot usually sustain a long period of contraction and require some rest between contractions. You can find skeletal muscles throughout your body and attached to most bones.

Cardiac muscles are only found in your heart. They share some similarities with skeletal muscles in that they appear striated, but they are set apart by three characteristics: *intercalated disks*, their branched appearance, and their single nucleus per cell. The intercalated disk connects two cardiac muscle fibers, end to end. Cardiac muscles contain only one nucleus in each cell, making them *mononucleate*, and they are *involuntary*, meaning you have no control over your cardiac muscles. You cannot stop your heart from beating or cause it to beat faster just by thinking about it. Cardiac muscles are able to beat consistently and not tire as easily as skeletal muscles. They beat constantly to pump blood throughout the body.

Smooth muscles also contract continually to move food and fluids through your digestive system. They are found in the hollow organs of the digestive system, in the uterus, and on the outside of vessels. Smooth muscles are involuntary and mononucleate like cardiac muscles, but they lack striations. In addition, smooth muscles are relatively short and are shaped like spindles, thus they are wider in the middle and come to points at the ends. In this experiment you will observe the three muscle types under the microscope and identify their structural characteristics.

Time Required

45 minutes

Materials

- ◉ microscope
- ◉ skeletal muscle slide
- ◉ cardiac muscle slide
- ◉ smooth muscle slide
- ◉ raw steak from grocery store
- ◉ raw beef or pork heart from grocery store
- ◉ raw beef or pork stomach or intestines from grocery store
- ◉ 3 microscope slides
- ◉ gloves

- 3 cover slips
- forceps
- scalpel
- pipette
- crayons or colored pencils
- small beaker of water or access to a sink
- science notebook

> **Safety Note** Wear gloves when handling raw meat. Wash your hands and all the surfaces touched by meat when you are finished. Be careful with the scalpel. Please review and follow the safety guidelines at the beginning of this volume.

Procedure

1. Place the skeletal muscle slide on the microscope and observe it under low power. Make a sketch of the tissue in your notebook. Label it "low power" and note any structures you can use for identification.

2. Observe the same muscle tissue under high power. Make another sketch of the tissue in your science notebook. Label it "high power" and note any additional structures you can use for identification. Be sure to locate the nucleus.

3. Repeat steps 1 and 2 using cardiac muscle and smooth muscle.

4. Prepare a wet mount of the raw skeletal muscle tissue. Figure 2 shows the technique for making a wet mount slide. To do so, tease off a tiny piece of steak using forceps. Use the scalpel to separate the meat into very small sections. Place a very small sample of meat on the slide, add a drop of water to the meat sample, and cover with a cover slip. In your science notebook, write down any visual similarities and differences between your wet mount and the prepared slide.

5. Repeat step 4 using raw cardiac and smooth muscle tissues.

6. Repeat steps 1 and 2 with each of the three wet mounts you prepared.

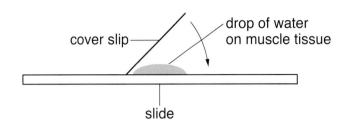

Figure 2

Analysis

1. Draw and color each of the three types of muscle tissue in the spaces provided below. Use the prepared microscope slides as references, for your drawings. Be sure to color your pictures accurately.

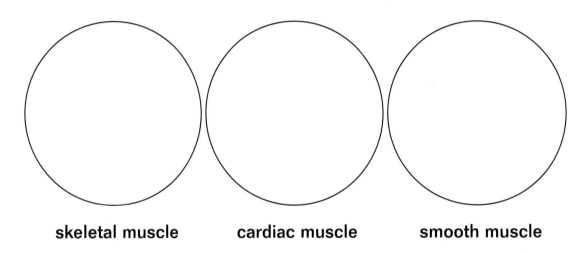

skeletal muscle   **cardiac muscle**   **smooth muscle**

2. Complete the data table comparing the three types of muscle tissues on page 63. In the appropriate box, write the characteristic that fits each muscle tissue type.

3. Where was the nucleus found in each of the muscle tissue types? Why do you think the nucleus was located in that area?

4. How does the ability of cardiac, smooth, and skeletal muscles vary in terms of sustaining contractions?

5. How does the cell shape of the three muscle tissues help it function?

Data Table			
Characteristic	Skeletal Muscle	Cardiac Muscle	Smooth Muscle
General shape			
Striated or not			
Voluntary or involuntary			
Easily fatigued or can sustain long contractions			
Location in the body			

What's Going On?

The shapes of the different muscle tissues are essential to their function. The long fibers of the skeletal muscles allow for significant contraction of the individual muscle fibers or cells. The bands you saw in the tissue are the different *microfilaments* that move the muscle fibers. The culminating effects of each of the thousands of microfilaments cause the muscle to shorten and cause movement.

The cardiac muscles also have these bands, but their intercalated disks are special junctions between their cells that synronize the movement of the cells. They are branched to improve their communication and durability around the heart. When your brain tells your cardiac muscles to contract, they are all able to beat at the same time for maximum efficiency. Smooth muscle does not need to pull on bones or squeeze the heart, but it does need to squeeze your intestines and other hollow organs to move food and other substances through. Their small size and tapered shape are ideal for squeezing tubes like blood vessels. In order to improve efficiency, there are two or three layers of smooth muscles around each hollow organ. The oblique layer is the inner layer that is wrapped around and encircles the organ. The longitudinal layer is the outer layer that runs perpendicular to the circular layer and parallel to the organ itself. The circular layer is sandwiched between the other two. Figure 3 shows three layers surrounding the stomach.

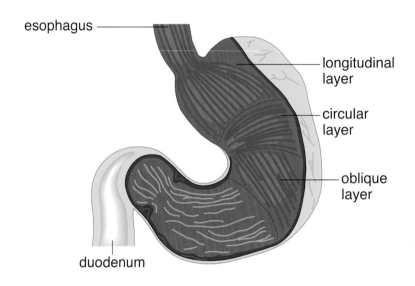

Figure 3

The stomach has three layers of muscle

Connections

All muscle tissue contracts to produce movement in your body, but different types of movements require different types of muscles. When you move your arm or leg you move skeletal muscles. Skeletal muscles are attached to your bones and pull on them like levers; muscles never push. For example, when you hold out your arm to show someone your muscles, you bring your hand toward your head. Your *brachialis* and *biceps brachii* muscles pull your *ulna*, a bone in your forearm, toward your body and move your forearm.

Cardiac muscles, however, do not pull on your bones like skeletal muscles. They are wrapped around your heart in a figure-8 pattern. These muscles are controlled by your *autonomic nervous system* and beat without you thinking about it. When they contract they squeeze your heart, forcing the blood to move through your heart and throughout your body.

Your cardiac muscles cannot pump all the blood alone, so smooth muscles help. There are smooth muscles around many of the major *arteries* that take oxygenated blood to your body. These smooth muscles are also wrapped around smaller arteries and squeeze in two different directions to move blood through them. The movement is similar to squeezing your fingers together while running your hand down a tube or water hose. As you squeeze the tube and move your hand down it, the water is forced out. The same kind of process occurs in your organs to move food through your digestive system.

Want to Know More?

See appendix for Our Findings.

Further Reading

"How a muscle contraction is signalled," 2009. YouTube. Available online. URL: http://www.youtube.com/watch?v=CepeYFVqmk4. Accessed October 24, 2009. The parts of a muscle sarcomere are explained on this teacher-produced video.

Kimball, John W. "Muscles," 2009. Kimball's Biology Pages. Available online. URL: http://users.rcn.com/jkimball.ma.ultranet/BiologyPages/M/Muscles.html. Accessed October 24, 2009. The author discusses the three types of muscle tissue and associated disorders.

University of Guelph, Developmental Biology Online. "Muscle Tissue." Available online. URL: http://www.uoguelph.ca/zoology/devobio/210labs/muscle1.html. Accessed October 20, 2009. This Web page gives information of the three muscle tissue types and includes labeled pictures of the tissues as seen under a microscope.

10. Lactose Intolerance

Topic

Many adults cannot digest the sugar lactose.

Introduction

Milk is one of the favorite foods of children. However, many adults suffer from cramps and diarrhea if they drink milk. These adults are described as *lactose intolerant* because they are unable to break down and digest lactose, a sugar. Why are some adults unable to digest lactose? The answer can be found at the genetic level.

Lactose is made up of two simple sugars, glucose and galactose, that are chemically joined (see Figure 1). Most people have the gene for producing lactase, the enzyme that breaks down lactose into glucose and galactose. These two simple sugars are easily digested by humans of all ages. As some people age, their lactase gene stops working, making it impossible for them to digest milk and milk products. As a result, the lactose molecules reach their large intestines (see Figure 2) intact and cause water to be drawn into the intestine. This water can cause intestinal cramps and watery diarrhea, which can be very uncomfortable. In addition, bacteria that live in the large intestine begin to use lactose as food. As they digest the sugar, they produce gas, which causes bloating and further discomfort. In this experiment, you will find out what kinds of foods contain lactose and how lactase breaks down lactose.

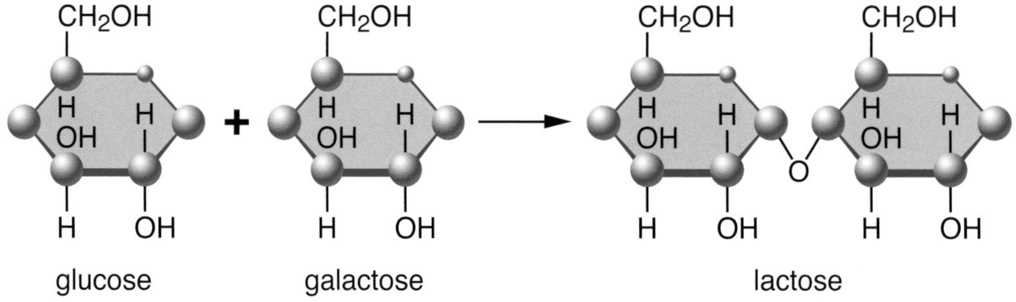

Figure 1

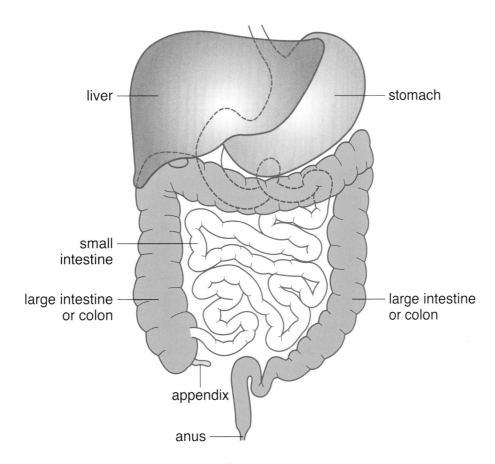

liver — stomach

small intestine

large intestine or colon — large intestine or colon

appendix

anus —

Figure 2

Time Required

45 minutes

Materials

- variety of milk products (such as whole milk, cottage cheese, yogurt, ice cream)
- lactose-free milk
- lactase tablet dissolved in a few milliliters of water
- glucose test strips
- glucose solution
- masking tape or labels
- waterproof pen
- well plate

- toothpicks
- science notebook

Procedure, Part A

1. Label one well of a well plate as "glucose." Label a second well as "lactose-free milk."

2. Label the other wells with the names of the milk products you have available. (You probably will not use all of the wells.)

3. Copy the data table in your science notebook, making enough rows for the milk products you are using. Write the names of these milk products on the data table.

4. Answer Analysis question 1.

5. Dip a glucose test strip in the glucose solution. Notice the changes to the test strip, which represent a positive test for glucose. Indicate the positive test for glucose by writing a "+" in the correct row of the data table.

6. Dip a glucose test strip into the milk containing lactase. Record the results on the data table.

7. Dip a different glucose test strip into each of the milk products in the well plate. Record whether or not the products contain glucose on the data table.

Data Table		
Food samples	**Part A: Glucose present (+) or absent (-)**	**Part B: Glucose present(+) or absent (-)**
Glucose solution		NA
Milk containing lactose		

Procedure, Part B

1. On the well plate, circle the labels of the milk products that *did not* test positive for glucose.

2. To each circled milk product, add one or two drops of lactase.

3. Gently stir the wells with toothpicks, using a clean toothpick for each well.

4. Answer Analysis question 2.

5. After 2 or 3 minutes, check each of the circled milk products for the presence of glucose. Record your findings in the third column of the data table. Write NA beside the products that are not being tested in part B.

6. Take a survey of your classmates to find out how many suffer discomfort when they drink milk.

7. Answer Analysis questions 3 through 5.

Analysis

1. Which of the products do you think will contain glucose?

2. Which of the circled products do you think will contain glucose?

3. How did lactase change the milk and milk products?

4. How many of your classmates are lactose intolerant? What percentage of the class do they represent?

5. Like all enzymes, lactase is a protein. How might heating lactase have changed the results of this experiment?

What's Going On?

In this experiment, you tested milk and milk products for the presence of glucose. If you used test strips that show the percentage of glucose present, you might have noticed that milk contains little or no glucose. Some of the milk products you tested might have contained some glucose. After you identified the products that contain no glucose, you added lactase. This enzyme converts the *disaccharide* sugar lactose into two *monosaccharides*, glucose and galactose. Both of these are easy to digest. The lactose-free milk was treated with lactase before it was packaged and sold. Glucose test strips dipped in the lactose-free milk showed a high level of glucose. The regular milk showed similar levels of glucose after it was treated with lactase.

Connections

Most adults are lactose intolerant, unable to digest the sugar in milk. People whose heritage can be traced to Eskimos, American Indians, sub-Saharan Africans, and people from the Mediterranean, Near East, Asia, and Pacific islands fall into this group. There is a correlation between individuals who are descended from dairy agriculturalists, such as the Arabs of Saudi Arabia, and the ability to tolerate lactose. The largest group of lactose tolerant adults is those descended from Northern Europeans, which includes many Americans. Scientists think that some time in human history, a mutation occurred that prevented the gene that turns off lactose tolerance from operating. These people would have had an advantage because they could consume milk when other foods were not available. This would have helped them survive.

No one knows for sure why the lactose intolerance gene developed in the first place. Some scientists speculate that the gene appeared a long time ago, maybe as long as 75 million years. It may have facilitated the weaning of children, making milk consumption uncomfortable for older offspring who might compete with newborns for milk. Another idea is that lactose malabsorption prevented adults from competing with infants for their only source of food.

Want to Know More?

See appendix for Our Findings.

Further Reading

"Lactose Intolerance," June 2009. National Digestive Diseases Information Clearing House. Available online. URL: http://digestive.niddk.nih.gov/ddiseases/pubs/lactoseintolerance/. Accessed October 24, 2009. Causes, symptoms, diagnosis, and treatment of lactose intolerance are discussed on this Web page.

ScienceDaily. "Lactose Intolerance Linked to Ancestral Environment," June 2, 2005. Available online. URL: http://www.sciencedaily.com/releases/2005/06/050602012109.htm. Accessed October 24, 2009. This article explains that people whose ancestors lived in regions where dairy farming was important are more likely to be able to digest lactose than those whose ancestors came from regions that did not support dairy farming.

TeenHealth. "Lactose Intolerance," 2009. Nemours Foundation. Available online. URL: http://kidshealth.org/teen/food_fitness/nutrition/lactose_intolerance.html. Accessed May 17, 2010. Written for teens, this Web page discusses the problems caused by lactose intolerance and explains how to keep some dairy products in the diet.

WebMD. "Lactose Intolerance—Topic Overview," Digestive Disorder Health Center, August 2009. Avaiable online. URL: http://www.webmd.com/digestive-disorders/tc/lactose-intolerance-topic-overview. Accessed February 13, 2010. This Web site explains the causes and symptoms of lactose intolerance.

11. Reaction Time

Topic

Distractions increase the time it takes to perceive and respond to a stimulus.

Introduction

Reaction time is the time it takes you to perceive something and react to it. For example, if you are driving down the road and the car in front of you stops suddenly, you stop. But before you do, several events occur. First, your senses perceive the stimulus, in this case the car that stops in front of you. The second event is recognition, the time it takes you to realize that a car has stopped. During this time, you apply information that is stored in your memory to the present situation. Situational awareness, the time it takes you to realize the meaning of what you are seeing, is the third event. You know that if you do not stop, you will hit the car. The fourth stage is response selection; you decide what to do. This is the time required for your brain to decide that you need to stop. The last stage is implementation; your brain sends a signal to your foot to step on the brakes, then you actually pick up your foot and move it.

Because reactions happen very quickly, you will not be able to break apart the components of a reaction in this experiment. Instead you will take one measurement that will encompass all these steps. Once you learn to measure reaction time, you will develop a hypothesis and carry out an experiment to see how one factor affects reaction time.

 Time Required

55 minutes

 Materials

- ↦ meterstick
- ↦ stopwatch

Safety Note
Please review and follow the safety guidelines at the beginning of this volume.

Procedure

1. Work with a partner to learn how to measure a person's reaction time. To do so, stand on a chair and hold a meterstick near the 100-centimeter end, letting the meterstick hang down. Have your partner hold his or her hand at the bottom of the meterstick in a "grab" position, close to, but not touching, the meterstick (see Figure 1). Tell your partner that you will drop the meterstick and you want him or her to catch it as fast as possible. (Do not tell your partner when you will drop the meterstick.) Without warning, drop the meterstick and record the place (in centimeters) where your partner caught it. For best results, retest the person's reaction time at least three times and average your results.

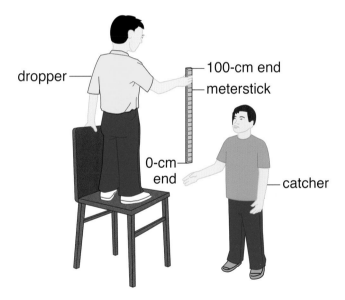

dropper — 100-cm end

meterstick

0-cm end

catcher

Figure 1

2. Convert the place on the meterstick to reaction time. You can do this in either of two ways. The simplest way is to refer to Data Table 1.

   The more precise way is to use the following formula:

   $$t = \sqrt{\frac{2y}{g}}$$

   where t equals time (in seconds), y is distance (in centimeters), and g is acceleration due to gravity, (980 cm/sec^2).

Data Table 1	
Place (cm)	**Time (sec)**
5	0.10 sec
10	0.14 sec
15	0.17 sec
20	0.20 sec
25.5	0.23 sec
30.5	0.25 sec
43	0.30 sec
61	0.35 sec
79	0.40 sec
99	0.45 sec

3. Now that you know how to measure a person's reaction time, your job is to design an experiment to find out how one factor affects reaction time. For example, you could see if a person's reaction time is affected by music, noise, dim light, or conversation. Or, you might want to find out how the reaction times of a group of teenagers compare to a group of people more than 40 years of age.

4. Answer Analysis questions 1 and 2.

5. Write the steps you plan to take (your experimental procedure) and the materials you plan to use (materials list) on Data Table 2. You can use any of the supplies provided by your teacher. Show your procedure and materials list to the teacher to find out if the procedure is acceptable and the materials you plan to use (material list) are available.

6. If you get teacher approval, carry out your experiment. If not, modify your work and show it to your teacher again.

7. Collect your results on a data table of your own design.

8. Answer Analysis questions 3 through 6.

Data Table 2	
Your experimental procedure	
Your materials list	
Teacher's approval	

Analysis

1. What factor will you test in your experiment?
2. Write a hypothesis stating what you expect to find in your experiment.
3. Did your hypothesis prove to be correct?
4. Why is it important that the person catching the meterstick not know when you are going to release it?
5. What conclusions can you draw from your experiment?
6. If you were going to do this experiment again, how would you improve it?

What's Going On?

In this experiment, the visual stimulus was the falling ruler. Once your eyes sent the signal to your brain that the ruler was falling, your brain had to recognize the ruler, determine what to do about it, then send a message to your hand to grab it. All of these processes took time.

Reaction times are influenced by one's level of alertness. As the driver of a car, you may be worried about the possibility of the car in front of you braking, so you are alert. Studies have shown than an alert driver can go through all of the steps of reaction in about 0.7 seconds. If you are not alert, reaction time is slower, dropping to about 1.25 seconds. The increased time is due to the fact that it takes longer for you to perceive the problem. In cases of surprise, reaction time is even slower. For example, you are driving down the road and a person steps in front of you. Perception time lengthens because your brain has to interpret this unusual event. In addition, you may try to decide the best course of action: should you brake or try to swerve? In total, it can take you 1.5 seconds to respond to this type of event.

Connections

Drivers need to be alert at all times. Distractions in the car are one of the leading causes of automobile crashes. Generally, young people have faster reaction times than older adults. However, a study by Professor David Strayer of the University of Utah has demonstrated that teen drivers who are using cell phones, like the driver in Figure 2, react as slowly to the brake lights of the car in front of them as 70-year-old drivers. In general, talking on the phone reduced teens' reaction time by 18 percent. In this study, Strayer got the same results with hand-held and hands-free phones. The important factor was that the teen drivers were dividing their attention between driving and talking. In another study, Strayer and his colleague associate professor Frank Drews found that teens on the phone are as impaired as drunk drivers. Other researchers have reached the same conclusions. In general, multitasking increases your chances of having a wreck.

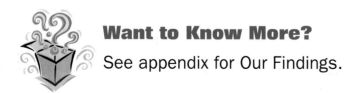

Want to Know More?

See appendix for Our Findings.

Figure 2

Talking on the phone slows your reaction time and increases the risk of a crash.

Further Reading

Associated Press. "Traffic jam? Blame cell phone users," 2009. Available online. URL: http://articles.moneycentral.msn.com/News/ TrafficJamBlameCellPhoneUsers.aspx. Accessed October 25, 2009. Dr. David Strayer explains how use of the cell phone affects driving.

Kosinski, Robert J. "A Literature Review on Reaction Time," August 2009. Available online. ULR: http://biae.clemson.edu/bpc/bp/Lab/110/ reaction.htm. Accessed October 25, 2009. Kosinski of Clemson University summarizes some important literature on reaction time.

Whitney, Lance. "Road test shows texting slows reaction time," June 25, 2009. Available online. URL: http://news.cnet. com/8301-1035_3-10272628-94.html. Accessed October 25, 2009. Studies from several sources confirm that texting while driving slows reaction time, increasing the chances of a crash.

12. Diagnosis of Blood Diseases

Topic

Examination of blood cells can help diagnose blood diseases.

Introduction

Blood, the only liquid tissue, is made up of two components: *plasma* and *formed elements*. The formed elements are cells and cell fragments. The most numerous cells in blood, *erythrocytes* or red blood cells (see Figure 1), are small, red disks that contain *hemoglobin*, a protein that binds to oxygen. *Platelets* are tiny fragments of cells that are essential for clotting.

Leukocytes, or white blood cells, are much larger than erythrocytes and function to protect the body from bacteria and viruses. Leukocytes are classified by the absence or presence of granules in their cytoplasm. Granulocytes include *neutrophils, eosinophils,* and *basophils*. Neutrophils, which have multilobed nuclei, act as *phagocytes* at sites on infection, attacking and consuming bacteria and cell debris. Eosinophils, cells that appear red when stained, are active against allergies and parasitic worms. Cells that take up a blue stain, the basophils, release *histamine*,

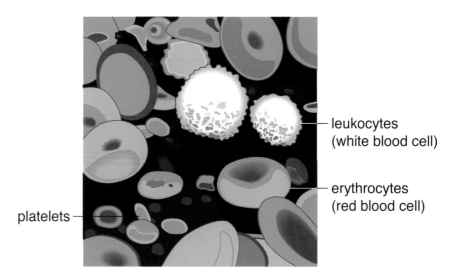

Figure 1

a chemical that causes tissue to become inflamed. Agranulates, cells that lack granules in the cytoplasm, include *lymphocytes* and *monocytes*. Lymphocytes have extremely large nuclei that almost fill the entire cells. These cells play important roles in immune responses. Monocytes, the largest leukocytes, fight chronic infection.

In this experiment, you are playing the role of a lab assistant. You accidentally dropped a box of blood slides, the case histories that accompany the slides, and the diagnoses of diseases shown on the slides. Your job is to match the correct slide to the case history and diagnosis.

Time Required

40 minutes

Materials

- access to an anatomy and physiology text or to the Internet
- science notebook

Safety Note   Please review and follow the safety procedures at the beginning of this volume.

Procedure

1. Examine Slide 1 (Figure 2), which shows normal blood cells. Count the number of erythrocytes, leukocytes, and platelets and record them on the data table. This will tell you how many of these formed elements are normally found in blood.

2. Examine Slide 2 (Figure 2). Count the number of erythrocytes, leukocytes, and platelets and record them on the data table.

3. Read the case histories of each blood disease or condition. Based on the case histories and the cells seen on the slide, write the letter of the case (A through F) on the data table.

4. Using your anatomy book or the Internet, find descriptions of the diseases or conditions described in the list of diagnoses. Then match information gathered from the slide and the case history to the correct diagnosis. Write the diagnosis on the data table.

5. Repeat steps 2 through 4 for the other slides and case histories.

Data Table					
Slide	**Erythrocytes**	**Leukocytes**	**Platelets**	**Case History**	**Diagnosis**
1				NA	Normal
2					
3					
4					
5					
6					
7					

Case Histories

Case History A. The patient is a 21-year-old female who has felt unusually tired and weak for the last several months. Her hands and feet are cold, and some days she feels dizzy and short of breath. Her red blood cell count is low.

Case History B. A 13-year-old male feels tired and has frequent headaches. His hands and feet are usually cold, and he experiences frequent episodes of extreme chest pain. His red blood cell count is low, and some of his erythrocytes are misshapen and clumped.

Case History C. A 45-year-old obese man has severe pain and swelling in one leg. He smokes a pack of cigarettes every day. Blood tests show a large number of platelets and a slower-than-normal clotting time.

Case History D. A 32-year-old female experiences frequent headaches, dizziness, and blurred vision. She reports chest pain on the previous day. Blood works shows that she has abnormally high levels of erythrocytes, leukocytes, and platelets.

Case History E. A 16-year-old male presents with numerous dark spots on the skin and several large bruises. He has been experiencing headaches, fever, fatigue, and occasional diarrhea. Blood work shows a low platelet count, low erythrocyte count, and some fragmented erythrocytes.

Case History F. A 28-year-old female has a fever, headache, and frequent nosebleeds. Her blood work reveals a low erythrocyte count and elevated number of leukocytes.

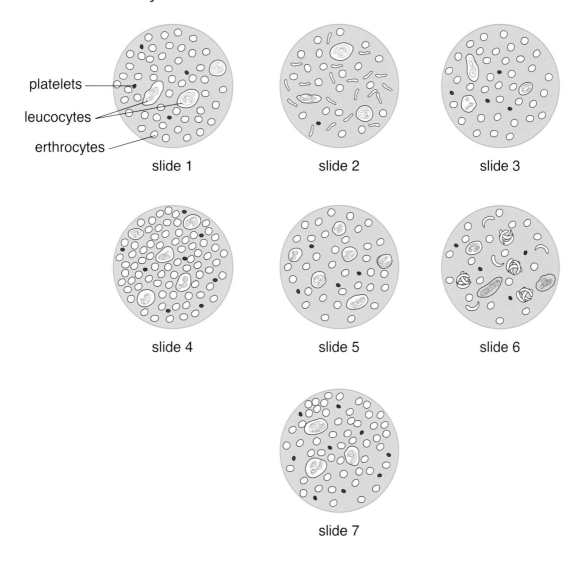

Figure 2

Diagnoses

- Iron deficiency anemia
- Sickle-cell anemia
- Excessive clotting disorder
- Thrombotic thrombocytopenic purpura
- Leukemia
- Polycythemia vera

Analysis

1. What is the function of erythrocytes? What protein in erythrocytes gives them their characteristic red color?

2. What is the function of leukocytes?

3. If a patient has a runny nose, cough, and fever, would you expect their leukocyte count to be higher or lower than normal? Explain your reasoning.

4. Why might a patient need a transfusion of platelets?

5. From the slides you observed, how are iron deficiency anemia and sickle-cell anemia similar?

6. Some of the erythrocytes in Slide 2 look smaller than usual. What is wrong with them?

7. Slide 4 has an abnormally large number of cells and platelets. How might this cause pain?

What's Going On?

Blood diseases can cause a myriad of symptoms. Examining a patient's blood helps a medical practitioner get to the root of the problem. *Anemia* is a general term for a condition in which there are not enough healthy erythrocytes to carry oxygen to all parts of the body. Iron-deficiency anemia can be due to a lack of iron or folic acid in the diet; both nutrients are required to make red blood cells. In *sickle-cell anemia*, some of the red blood cells are distorted, and therefore unable to carry oxygen. In addition, these cells can clump and block the flow of blood through small vessels. Other types of anemia include *aplastic anemia*, in which the bone marrow does not make enough red blood cells, and *hemolytic anemia,* in which blood cells are prematurely destroyed.

Excessive clotting disorder can be inherited or acquired. In the acquired form, some other disease or disorder prompts clotting. For example, a person who has narrow or damaged blood vessels may experience unwanted clotting. Clots are dangerous because they can block vessels. Organs that do not receive blood can be damaged.

A person with polycythemia vera, a condition in which the body makes too many red blood cells, may be unaware of the condition for years. Even though their blood is thicker than normal, symptoms do not arise until some areas of the body do not receive adequate blood flow. Thick blood moves slowly and is more likely to produce clots than thin blood. One complication of slow-moving blood is pain in any region of the body, including the heart.

In thrombotic thrombocytopenic purpura, blood clots form in small vessels due to clumping of platelets. With the platelets tied up in abnormal clots, there are not enough circulating in the blood to seal small breaks in blood vessels. As a result, bleeding occurs in the skin producing small dark patches, *purpura*. More extensive and dangerous bleeding can occur, especially in the brain and kidneys.

Leukemia is cancer of the white blood cells. The cancerous cells are abnormal, so cannot carry out the functions of white blood cells. These cells grow in number at an accelerated rate, and they live a long time. Eventually, there are so many abnormal leukocytes that they crowd out normal white blood cells, erythrocytes, and platelets.

Connections

Medical practitioners rely on blood tests to provide them with clues about their patients' conditions. A complete blood count, or CBC, measures the number of erythrocytes, leukocytes, and platelets. It also provides a *hematocrit*, a measure of the amount of space occupied by erythrocytes. A high hematocrit could indicate dehydration while a low one might suggest anemia or some other blood disease. A CBC also includes a mean corpuscular volume (MCV) that measures the average size of erythrocytes. Abnormally small cells could indicate a blood disease.

The basic metabolic panel (BMP) provides information about blood chemistry as well as the heart, muscles, bones, kidneys, and liver. The blood glucose test lets you know if you have normal levels of sugar in your blood. Abnormally high levels are an indicator of diabetes. High levels of calcium in the blood could be due to diseases of kidneys, bone, or the thyroid gland. Electrolytes, the minerals in blood, include chloride, bicarbonate, and sodium. If levels of electrolytes are off, your practitioner might suspect dehydration or a more serious problem with the heart or liver.

Information about the overall health of the cardiovascular system comes from tests that check your blood levels of cholesterol. People with abnormally high levels of cholesterol are at risk of a heart attack. Tests of blood enzyme levels can provide information about the heart and other organs. *Creatine kinase* (CK) is an enzyme that leaks out of heart muscle when it is damaged. High levels of CK and similar enzymes might indicate a heart attack. Another indicator of heart attack is high levels of the muscle protein *troponin*.

Want to Know More?

See appendix for Our Findings.

Further Reading

"Anemia," 2009. KidsHealth. Available online. URL: http://kidshealth.org/parent/medical/heart/anemia.html. Accessed October 30, 2009. Several types of anemia are explained on this Web site in simple language.

"Components of Blood," August 2006. Merck Manuals. Available online. URL: http://www.merck.com/mmhe/sec14/ch169/ch169b.html. Accessed November 27, 2009. This Web page includes pictures of the various types of blood cells, as well as explanation of their functions.

Information Center for Sickle Cell and Thalassemic Disorders. Available online. URL: http://sickle.bwh.harvard.edu/index.html. Accessed October 30, 2009. The authors are medical experts who explain blood diseases and the basic science behind those diseases.

Mayo Clinic. "Sickle Cell Anemia," 2009. Available online. URL: http://www.mayoclinic.com/health/sickle-cell-anemia/DS00324. Accessed October 30, 2009. Staffers at Mayo clinic explain the symptoms, causes, and treatment of sickle-cell anemia.

13. Exercise, Pulse, and Recovery Rate

Topic

Pulse rate and rate of recovery vary among individuals and depend on the level of physical activity.

Introduction

The heart is the pump in your cardiovascular system that sends blood through the body. This pump has four chambers: two small *atria* and two larger, stronger *ventricles*. Deoxygenated blood flows into the right atrium from the body, then drains into the right ventricle, and is pumped to the lungs. The left atrium receives oxygenated blood from the lungs, which drains into the left ventricle and is pumped to tissues throughout the body. Each contraction of the left ventricle sends a high-pressure surge of blood into the arteries, causing the arterial walls to stretch. The rhythmic expansion of arteries in response to blood flow is the *pulse*. By measuring the pulse, one can measure the heart rate. Pulse can be *palpated*, or felt, at several pressure points (see Figure 1) by placing two fingers on the points and applying gentle pressure. Your pulse varies depending on age and level of activity. In this experiment, you will design a procedure to find out how pulse rate varies among individuals with different levels of activity. You will also find out how long it takes for pulse to recover its resting rate after exercise.

Time Required

15 minutes for Part A
45 minutes for Part B

Materials

- ➾ stopwatch
- ➾ access to an open area (indoors or outdoors)
- ➾ science notebook

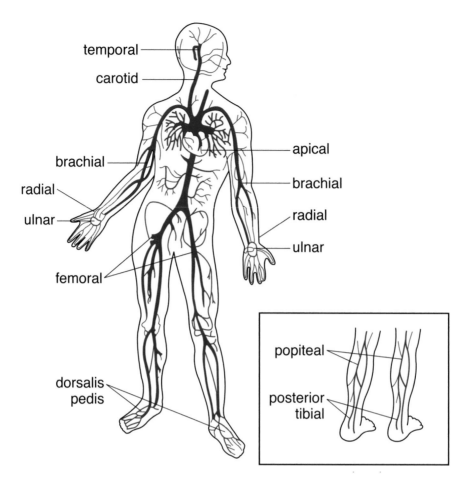

Figure 1

Pressure points can be found at several locations on the body. The most commonly used pressure points are the radial and carotid.

Safety Note Do not perform this experiment if you have a health condition that prevents you from participating in vigorous physical activity. Please review and follow the safety guidelines at the beginning of this volume.

Procedure, Part A

1. Take your resting radial pulse. To do so, turn your right arm so that the hand is palm up. Place the first two fingers of your left hand on the outer crease of the right wrist (see Figure 2). Start the stopwatch. Count the number of pulses for 15 seconds. Multiply the count by 4 to find the pulse rate per minute. Record your finding on Data Table 1.

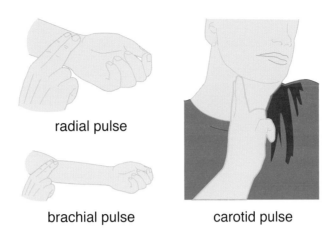

Figure 2

Finding your pulse

2. Take your resting brachial pulse. To do so, rest your right arm on a table or desk, palm up, and slightly bent at the elbow. Place the first two fingers of the left hand in the depression found about 1/2 inch [in.] (1.25 centimeter [cm]) above the crease on the inside of the elbow (see Figure 2). Start the stopwatch. Count the number of pulses for 15 seconds. Multiply the count by 4 and record your finding on Data Table 1.

3. Take your resting carotid pulse. To do so, place two fingers on your neck on either side of the neck (see Figure 2). Start the stopwatch. Count the number of pulses for 15 seconds. Multiply the count by 4 and record your finding on Data Table 1.

4. Average all three pulses to find your average pulse. Record your average resting pulse on Data Table 1.

Data Table 1				
	Radial pulse	**Brachial pulse**	**Carotid pulse**	**Average resting pulse**
Resting				

Procedure, Part B

1. Your job is to design and perform an experiment that has the following two functions:

   a. Compare your heart rate to the heart rates of three other students under the following conditions:

   After walking for three minutes

   After jogging in place for three minutes

   After performing jumping jacks for three minutes

   b. Compare your recovery time after each exercise to the recovery time of the same three students. Recovery time is how long it takes your heart to return to its resting rhythm.

2. Before you conduct your experiment, decide exactly what you are going to do. Write the steps you plan to take (your experimental procedure) on Data Table 2. As you are designing the experiment, keep these points in mind:

   a. Pulse rate should be measured immediately after physical activity.

   b. Between activities, give your pulse time to return to its resting rate.

   c. Everyone in the group should perform physical activities to the same level of intensity.

Data Table 2	
Your experimental procedure	
Teacher's approval	

3. Show your procedure to your teacher. If you get teacher approval, proceed with your experiment. If not, modify your work and show it to your teacher again.

4. Collect your results on a data table of your own design.

Analysis

1. What causes your pulse?
2. Where would you expect your pulse to be stronger, at your wrist or at your ankle? Explain your answer.
3. Which activity caused your pulse rate to increase the most?
4. What is the average resting pulse rate of students in your group?
5. What is recovery time?
6. Who would you expect to have the faster recovery time: an athlete or a nonathlete? Why?

What's Going On?

The pulse rate is the number of times you can feel the pulse in one minute. Since a pulse is created with each heart beat, the pulse rate is also the heart rate. Heart rate depends on a variety of things including age, health, and activity. The normal resting heart rate for different age groups is shown on Data Table 3.

A fast pulse rate, more than 100 beats per minute for an adult, is called *tachycardia*. Tachycardia occurs normally after exercise and can also be felt associated with strong emotions or pain. However long-term tachycardia may indicate heart disease. A slow pulse rate, less than 50 beats per minute for adults, is *bradycardia*. Chronic bradycardia is another indicator of certain diseases or problems with the heart.

During intense exercise, the heart rate normally increases to get plenty of oxygen to the cells and get rid of carbon dioxide that builds up from *cellular respiration*. After exercise, the heart beats fast for a short time as it continues to supply the needs of cells. As oxygen levels increase and carbon dioxide is cleared, the heart rate begins to drop; in a short time, the heart recovers its normal resting rate. Recovery time can give a rough estimation of a person's level of fitness. Because the heart is a muscle, aerobic exercise strengthens it. During running or other aerobic tasks, the heart handles larger-than-usual volumes of blood and as a result it becomes slightly larger. With each beat, the heart can then pump a greater volume of blood, making it more efficient. Because of its efficiency, the heart rate of an athlete will return to the resting rate faster than that of a nonathlete.

Data Table 3	
Age	**Heart beats per minute**
Newborns	120 to 160
Toddlers	90 to 150
Children	70 to 120
Adults	60 to 100

Connection

Medical practitioners check not only pulse rate but also other characteristics of the pulse. The strength of a pulse depends on the amount of blood forced into the arteries from the left ventricle. An unusually strong pulse is described as bounding and can be due to exercise, fear or anxiety, or alcohol consumption. A strong pulse, one that is stronger than normal but not as strong as bounding pulse, might indicate shock or bleeding. A weak pulse indicates that the ventricle is not pumping a large volume of blood. Causes of a weak pulse include dehydration, low blood pressure, and malnutrition.

The rhythm of a pulse should be regular. An irregular pulse is one in which the time between beats or the strength of beats may vary. An intermittent pulse is a type of irregular pulse in which the strength is normal but a beat is skipped occasionally. Figure 3 shows several kinds of pulse rates.

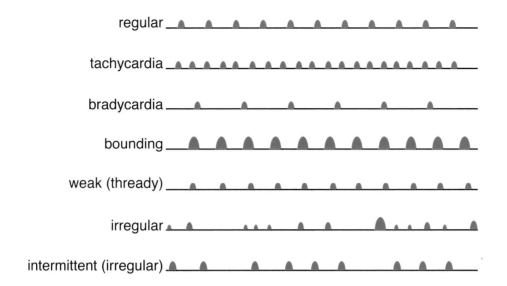

regular

tachycardia

bradycardia

bounding

weak (thready)

irregular

intermittent (irregular)

Figure 3

Pulse rates

Want to Know More?

See appendix for Our Findings.

Further Reading

"Bounding Pulse," 2009. HowStuffWorks. Available online. URL: http://healthguide.howstuffworks.com/pulse-bounding-dictionary.htm. Accessed October 31, 2009. The diagnostic tests and causes of bounding pulse are explained on this Web site.

"Heart Rate or Pulse," 2003. National Emergency Medicine Association (NEMA). Available online. URL: http://www.nemahealth.org/programs/healthcare/heart_rate_pulse.htm. Accessed October 31, 2009. This NEMA Web page explains how one can determine his or her target heart rate during exercise.

"Pulse Measurement," 2009. WebMD. Available online. URL: http://www.webmd.com/heart-disease/pulse-measurement. Accessed October 31, 2009. This Web site explains how to check your pulse and why you might choose to do so.

14. Male Reproductive System

Topic

Structures in the male reproductive system can be examined microscopically.

Introduction

The purpose of both male and female human reproductive systems is to produce *gametes*, haploid cells. Human gametes, ova and spermatozoa (sperm), are produced by *meiosis*, a type of cell division that reduces the usual chromosome number from 46 to 23. When an egg and sperm combine, the resulting cell contains the requisite 46 chromosomes. Meiosis occurs in specialized organs, the *gonads*.

In males, the gonads are *testes,* which are located in two external sacs that form the *scrotum*. The outermost layer of the testes is the capsule, a structure made of connective tissue. Inward extensions of the capsule, called *septa,* divide each testis into compartments or *lobules*. Within each lobule are the sperm-producing structures, long, coiled *seminiferous tubules. Interstitial cells* located between the tubules produce *testosterone,* the male hormone. In each lobule, the seminiferous tubules merge to form the rete testis, a straight tube. From here, sperm leave the testis and travel to the *epididymis,* a comma-shaped structure that hugs the surface of the testis. In the epididymis, sperm complete their period of maturation. Figure 1 shows the testis, epididymis, and a cross section of a seminiferous tubule with spermatozoa developing inside.

Time Required

55 minutes

Materials

- compound light microscope
- prepared slide of human (or mammal) testis

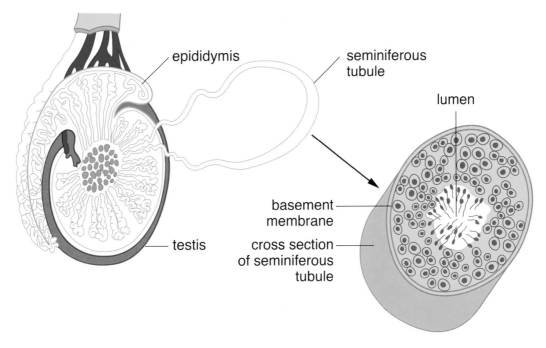

Figure 1

- prepared slide of sperm smear
- access to the Internet
- science notebook

Procedure

1. Observe a prepared slide of human (or mammal) testis.

   a. View the slide under low power. In your science notebook, sketch what you see and label the capsule and septa.

   b. Observe the slide under medium power. Using Figure 1 as a guide, find the small circles in each lobule. These are cross sections of seminiferous tubules. In your science notebook, sketch several seminiferous tubules.

   c. Observe one seminiferous tubule under high power. Locate the basement membrane and the lumen of the tubule. Label these structures on your drawing.

d. Focus on the cells within the tubule. *Sertoli cells* are large and pale with oval nuclei. The job of Sertoli cells is to surround and support the developing spermatozoa. Most of the cells are germ cells that are dividing to produce sperm. Cells nearest the basement membrane are *spermatogonia*, the *diploid* cells from which sperm are formed. Moving toward the lumen, cells are in various stages of development from *spermatocytes* to *spermatids* and finally *spermatozoa* (see Figure 2). On your drawing, label Sertoli cells, spermatogonia, and spermatozoa.

2. To check your drawings, access the images of "Male Reproductive System, Testis," at http://www.histol.chuvashia.com/atlas-en/male-01-en.htm. On this Web site, the structures and cells of the testis are labeled.

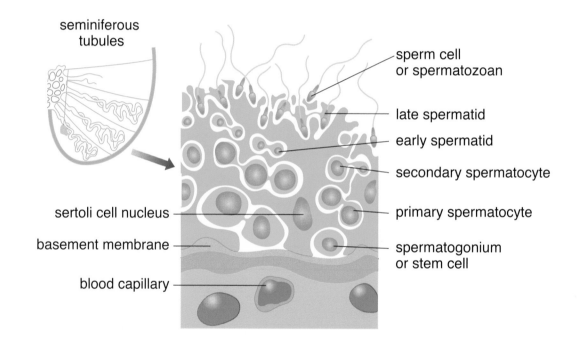

Figure 2

3. Observe a prepared slide of a sperm smear under low then medium or high power.

   a. Draw two or three sperm cells that have "normal," pear-shaped heads.

   b. Not all sperm in a specimen are normal. Look for misshapen sperm and draw three examples in your science notebook.

Analysis

1. How many chromosomes are found in most human cells? How many are found in sperm cells?

2. What process produces cells with a reduced chromosome number?

3. What are spermatogonia? Where are they located?

4. Sperm are cells, but they lack cytoplasm and most organelles. Why do you think sperm are different from other cells?

5. All sperm are not shaped the same. Describe the most common shape as well as two other shapes seen on the slide.

What's Going On?

The production of haploid sperm cells from diploid germ cells is *spermatogenesis*. The cells closest to the basement membrane are the germinal (or stem) cells, spermatogonia. These diploid cells are continuously undergoing mitosis, a type of cell division that produces daughter cells that have the same number of chromosomes as the original cell. Two types of daughter cells are produced: Type A cells, which take the place of the original cells, and Type B cells, the primary spermatocytes. Type B cells are pushed away from the basement membrane toward the lumen. Each primary spermatocyte undergoes the first stage of meiosis to produce two haploid secondary spermatocytes. Within a short time, these cells go through the second meiotic division to form spermatids, which are small, round cells. With each division, the cells are pushed closer to the lumen.

To become a cell that can swim, each spermatid undergoes *spermiogenesis*. In this process, the cell loses its cytoplasm and develops a flagellum. The resulting cell is a spermatozoa, made up only of a head containing DNA, a midpiece of mitochondria to provide energy, and a flagellum for swimming. Besides DNA, the head contains a sac of enzymes, the acrosome, that enable the sperm to break down the outer covering on the egg.

Sertoli or sustentacular cells found among the developing spermatozoa are joined tightly together to form a wall between the developing sperm and the seminiferous tubule, creating a blood-testes barrier. Because sperm are not formed until after puberty, the body's immune system would not recognize them as "self" and would form antibodies against them, destroying the cells. The barrier protects sperm from destruction by the immune system.

Connections

Infertility in males can stem from several problems. *Semen*, which is made of up sperm and the fluid surrounding it, can be analyzed to help identify the problem. The volume of semen is measured; normal volume ranges from 0.5 to 1.0 teaspoons (tsp) (2.5 to 5 milliliters [ml]). Abnormal semen volume could indicate problems with the glands that produce seminal fluids. The sperm concentration, the number of sperm per ml, is also measured. Most men produce about 20 million sperm per ml. Tests also look at the amount of fructose, a simple sugar, in semen. Fructose is the molecule that the mitochondria use to make energy. Fructose is provided in the epididymis, so its absence could point to an obstruction. Sperm motility, or ability to swim, is an important factor. In fertile males, at least 63 percent of the sperm are motile. The way in which sperm swim is also graded on a scale of 1 to 4, with 1 being slowest and 4 fastest. In addition, sperm morphology is examined. A large number of deformed sperm can prevent fertilization of the egg.

Further Reading

Gunin, Andrei. "Male Reproductive System, Testis," Histology Images, Histology for Medical Students, 2009. Available online. URL: http://www. histol.chuvashia.com/atlas-en/male-01-en.htm. Accessed October 31, 2009. This Web site provides very clear images of the testis, especially cells within the seminiferous tubules.

"Image Gallery," Veterinary Gamete Biology Laboratory. Available online. URL: http://www.vetmed.ucdavis.edu/apc/MeyersLab/Labsite%2003/ image%20gallery.html. Accessed October 31, 2009. The University of California, Davis, School of Veterinary Medicine provides excellent images of equine sperm.

King, David. "Testis," April 24, 2009. Available online. URL: http://www. siumed.edu/~dking2/erg/testis.htm. Accessed October 31, 2009. King of Southern Illinois University School of Medicine shares microscopic images of testis at various magnifications.

15. Female Reproductive System

Topic

Structures in the female reproductive system can be examined microscopically.

Introduction

The female reproductive system has two functions: to provide *gametes* and to nurture a developing embryo. Female gametes are *ova*, or egg cells, produced in the *ovaries*. After a female reaches puberty, she releases one ovum each month. The ovum develops in a tiny saclike structure, the *ovarian follicle*.

An ovary contains follicles in different stages of development. Each follicle holds an immature egg or *oocyte* and one or more layers of cells surrounding it. A *primordial follicle* is one that contains an oocyte surrounded by one layer of follicle cells. A *primary follicle* has two more layers of cells and a *secondary follicle* has developed a fluid-filled space called the *antrum*. The most mature stage, the *vesicular* or *graafian follicle*, bulges from the ovary's surface. The oocyte in this follicle is held in place by a stalk of tissue on one side of the antrum (see Figure 1).

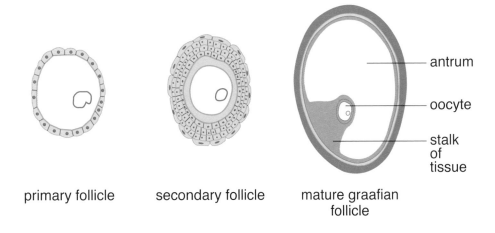

primary follicle   secondary follicle   mature graafian follicle

Figure 1

After *ovulation*, when the follicle erupts and the oocyte is released, the ruptured follicle develops into a different structure, the *corpus luteum*. The primary function of a corpus luteum is to release the female hormones *estrogen* and *progesterone*. If pregnancy does not occur, the corpus luteum begins to shrink after 10 or 12 days and forms a white scar. The corpus luteum remains functional if pregnancy does occur, providing the hormones needed to maintain the uterine lining to support the embryo.

After an oocyte is released from a follicle, it travels down a long tube, the *oviduct*, to the uterus. If the egg is fertilized, it begins a series of rapid cell divisions, then implants in the uterine wall. If *fertilization* does not occur, the egg passes out of the body during the next menstrual cycle. In this experiment, you will examine microscopic slides of ovarian tissue, oviducts, and vagina.

Time Required

55 minutes

Materials

- ➔ compound light microscope
- ➔ prepared microscope slide of cross section of the wall of mammalian uterus
- ➔ prepared microscope slide of cross section of oviduct
- ➔ prepared microscope slide of the wall of the vagina
- ➔ access to the Internet
- ➔ science notebook

Safety Note   **Please review and follow the safety guidelines at the beginning of this volume.**

Procedure

1. Observe a prepared slide of a cross section of the wall of a mammalian ovary.

   a. On low power, focus on an area of the slide that shows the outer edge of the ovary and some of the interior. The outer layer is made up of epithelial cells. Beneath these cells are groups of follicles containing oocytes at various stages of development. Oocytes appear as large cells with prominent, darkly stained nuclei. In your science notebook, draw several different follicles with their oocytes.

b. Move the slide so that you can survey several areas. Notice the different sizes of follicles throughout the ovary. The more mature follicles have a cavity that is filled with estrogen. Find and draw one or two of these mature follicles in your science notebook.

c. Continue to search the slide until you find a corpus luteum, which is a follicle that has erupted or broken open (see Figure 2). Draw a corpus luteum in your science notebook. Also locate and draw an ovarian scar, a small pit or white line where a corpus luteum has shrunk.

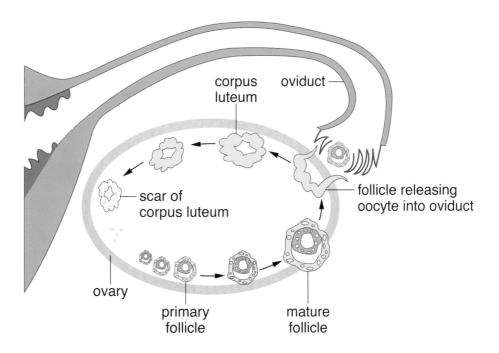

corpus luteum   oviduct

scar of corpus luteum

follicle releasing oocyte into oviduct

ovary

primary follicle

mature follicle

Figure 2

2. Observe a prepared slide of an oviduct.

a. View the slide on low power. Notice that the oviduct has two distinct regions: the outer layers of smooth muscles and the inner mucosa.

b. Move the slide so that you are looking at the mucosa and the lumen. Switch to medium power and examine the cells of the mucosa. Locate some ciliated cells. The job of these cells is to move the oocyte down the oviduct toward the uterus. Draw several cells of the mucosa.

3. Observe a prepared slide of the wall of the vagina.

    a. On low power, observe and draw the three layers of the vagina: mucosa, muscularis, and adventitia. The mucosa is the thin upper layer made of epithelial cells. The thickest layer is the muscularis, which is made up of an inner, circular layer of smooth muscle and an outer layer of longitudinal muscle. The outermost layer is the adventitia, which contains elastic fibers and adjoins loose connective tissue.

    b. Move the slide to the edge of the mucosa and switch to medium or high power. Observe and draw the cells that make up the mucosa. Notice that they are stratified squamous epithelial cells.

4. To check your drawings, access the images "Female Reproductive System, Ovary" at http://www.histol.chuvashia.com/atlas-en/female-01-en.htm and "Blue Histology-Female Reproductive System " at http://www.lab.anhb.uwa.edu.au/mb140/CorePages/FemaleRepro/FemaleRepro.htm#LabFollic. On these Web sites, the structures of ovaries, uterus, and vagina are shown and labeled.

Analysis

1. What type of cells makes up the outermost layer of an ovary?
2. Describe a primary follicle.
3. Describe a vesicular or graafian oocyte.
4. What is the function of the corpus luteum?
5. Why would the ovaries of a 40-year-old woman show numerous white scars?
6. Describe the epithelial cells that make up the vaginal mucosa.

What's Going On?

The production of haploid gametes, *oogenesis,* begins in a female before she is born. In the fetus, *oogonia*, the diploid stem cells in the ovaries, undergo mitosis and a period of growth. These cells then begin the first meiotic division, but do not complete it. They are surrounded by a layer of flattened cells, forming primordial follicles. At birth, a female has about 2 million primordial follicles in her ovaries.

These follicles exist in a state of suspended animation until puberty. During this time, some of the follicles are reabsorbed by the body, so that the total count drops to about 400,000. Each month, a few follicles are activated, but only one of the oocytes finishes meiosis I inside a Graafian follicle to form two haploid cells. Although each of these cells contains 23 chromosomes, they are very different. One of the cells, the first *polar body*, is very small because it has little cytoplasm. The larger cell, which received all of the cytoplasm, is the oocyte. It is released from the follicle during ovulation. The polar body undergoes meiosis II to form two smaller polar bodies that disintegrate and are reabsorbed by the body. The oocyte continues meiosis until it reaches metaphase II, where it stops. If it is not fertilized, this cell dies and is also reabsorbed. However if fertilization occurs, it completes meiosis II, forming the ovum and another tiny polar body. The nuclei of the ovum and sperm then combine in the process of fertilization.

Connections

Infertility in females can be caused by a variety of conditions including inadequate hormones, ovarian problems, blocked oviducts, or tumors in the uterus. One of the most common ovarian conditions is pelvic inflammatory disease (PID), a bacterial infection of one or more reproductive structures. Another disorder is polycystic ovary syndrome (PCO) in which the ovaries do not produce the hormones needed to cause follicle development. Instead, the follicles become fluid-filled cysts. Endometriosis is a condition in which sections of the uterine lining implant in the wrong places such as the oviducts or the ovaries. These patches of tissue form cysts that may become blisters and scars. Scarring can block the oviducts and prevent fertilization. Age also has a tremendous impact on fertility. At age 25, a woman having unprotected sex has a 25 percent chance of become pregnant. By age 40, this chance is reduced to 5 percent.

Want to Know More?

See appendix for Our Findings.

Further Reading

Histology World. Available online. URL: http://www.histology-world.com/ photoalbum/thumbnails.php?album=17. Accessed November 1, 2009. Histology World provides access to hundreds of beautiful slides, most with labels and explanations. Both the female and male reproductive systems are included in this collection.

King, David. "Ovary," April 24, 2009. Available online. URL: http://www. siumed.edu/~dking2/erg/testis.htm. Accessed October 31, 2009. King, of Southern Illinois University School of Medicine, shares microscopic images of the ovaries at various magnifications.

"What Causes Infertility in Women," Health-Cares.net, June 2005. Available online. URL: http://womens-health.health-cares.net/female-infertility-causes.php. Accessed November 1, 2009. This Web site explains how hormonal imbalances lead to infertility.

16. Vertebrae of the Neck

Topic

Structures of the vertebral column can be examined by dissecting a chicken neck.

Introduction

The human vertebral column or spine is part of the *axial skeleton*, the central core of the skeletal system. Other parts of the axial skeleton include the skull and thoracic cage. The vertebral column is made up of 26 bones that extend from the skull to the pelvis. These bones stack on top of each other and are grouped into three regions: cervical (seven bones), thoracic (twelve bones), and lumbar (five bones). Below the vertebral column, in the pelvis, are the sacrum, made of five fused bones, and the coccyx, composed of four fused bones (see Figure 1).

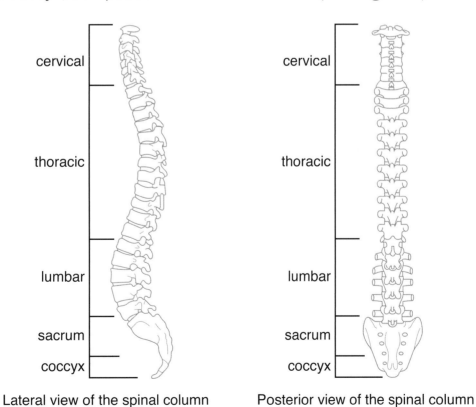

Lateral view of the spinal column   Posterior view of the spinal column

Figure 1

The vertebral column has several important jobs: It supports the trunk of the body and transmits the body's weight to the pelvic girdle and the legs. In addition, the vertebral column protects the spinal cord. It also provides points of attachment for muscles of the neck and back and for the ribs.

All of the vertebrae have similar characteristics (see Figure 2). The two main regions of a vertebra are the anterior, disc-shaped body, or *centrum*, and the posterior vertebral arch. A central column called the *vertebral foramen* passes through the arch. The arch is made up of two *pedicles* and two *laminae*. The pedicles, or "little feet," are short extensions from the centrum that create the sides of the arch. The laminae extend from the pedicles to form the arch. In addition, seven processes extend from the arch. The *spinous process* is in the middle and a *transverse process* extends from each side. Paired superior and inferior articular processes are covered in cartilage. Each of these two processes ends in a *facet*, a "little face," where one vertebra forms a joint with another vertebra.

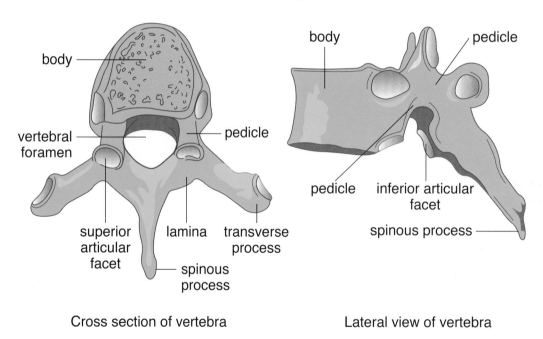

Cross section of vertebra   Lateral view of vertebra

Figure 2

Besides these general characteristics, vertebrae have their own unique qualities. The cervical vertebrae are the smallest. The body of a cervical vertebra is somewhat oval instead of round. The spinous process is relatively short and split at the tip. The seventh cervical vertebra is larger than the other six, and its process can be seen below the skin. In this experiment, you will examine the vertebrae of a chicken neck.

Time Required

40 minutes for Part A
50 minutes for Part B
50 minutes for Part C

Materials

- raw chicken neck
- scalpel
- forceps
- dissecting tray or paper towels
- beaker (200 to 400 milliliters [ml])
- hot plate
- hot mitts or oven mitts
- piece of wire, about 10 inches (in.) (25.4 centimeters [cm]) long
- colored pencils or crayons
- science notebook

> **Safety Note**   Take care when working with scalpels and the hot plate. Use hot mitts. Wash your hands and all work surfaces after working with chicken. Please review and follow the safety guidelines at the beginning of this volume.

Procedure, Part A

1. Place the raw chicken neck on a dissecting tray or paper towels.
2. Examine the neck to see if you can identify the skin and muscle tissue.
3. Use the scalpel and forceps to remove as much skin and muscle as possible from the vertebrae. As you do, notice how the muscle is attached to each vertebra.
4. Thread the wire through the vertebral foramens of the vertebrae so that they cannot get separated during part B of the procedure.

Procedure, Part B

1. Place the chicken neck in a beaker of water.

2. Heat the water and chicken neck on a hot plate for about 40 minutes.

3. Use hot mitts to remove the beaker from the hot plate.

4. Use forceps to remove the chicken neck from the hot water. Place the chicken neck on the dissecting tray or paper towels to cool.

Procedure, Part C

1. Use the scalpel and forceps to remove any remaining tissue from the vertebral bones.

2. Clean the bones under running water.

3. Examine each vertebra. Locate the following structures on one or more vertebra and point them out to your teacher:

   a. spinous process   e. pedicle

   b. transverse process   f. lamina

   c. vertebral foramen   g. superior articular process

   d. body   h. inferior articular process

Analysis

1. How many vertebrae are in the chicken neck?

2. How do vertebrae protect the spinal cord?

3. Color the following structures in the generalized cervical vertebra in Figure 3:

   superior articular facet—red   pedicle—blue

   lamina—green   transverse process—purple

   spinous process—yellow   vertebral foramen—gray

   body—orange

4. Where do muscles attach to vertebrae?

5. Where do vertebrae attach to other vertebrae?

6. Are all of the vertebrae in a chicken neck identical? If not, how did they vary?

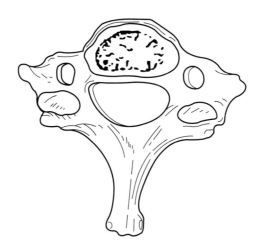

Figure 3
Cervical vertebra

What's Going On?

Just like the human neck, the chicken neck is designed to protect the delicate tissue of the spinal cord. Chickens have longer necks than humans, with 12 to 14 vertebrae. The necks are long to provide flexibility and to cushion the brain from shock when the bird is walking. Chickens also use their necks to help with balance when walking and perching. Although chickens do little flying, they are capable of flight and have a light-weight, porous skeleton similar to most birds. The inside of the bones have numerous open spaces, similar to the *spongy bone* of humans. Spongy bone can withstand forces from many directions and provides a good foundation for muscle attachment. Some of the vertebrae in chicken necks are fused, an adaptation that provides stability during flight.

Connections

Before birth, the human vertebral column is made up of 33 separate bones. Nine of these bones eventually fuse to form the sacrum and coccyx. A newborn has a C-shaped spine. However, as a child grows and begins to walk, the adult S-shaped spine develops. The spine's shape makes it flexible and prevents severe jarring of the skull when we walk or run.

Between the vertebrae are pads called *intervertebral discs*. Each pad is made up of a tough outer layer of *fibrocartilage* and an elastic central mass. The pads help cushion the individual vertebrae and absorb shock.

The intervertebral discs are very spongy in young people, but they become drier and less able to compress with age. The drying of disc pads, and weakening of ligament support along the spine, can lead to *herniated discs,* a bulging or breaking of the disc. Depending on their locations, herniated discs can cause numbness or weakness in limbs, or pain in the limbs or low back.

Want to Know More?

See appendix for Our Findings.

Further Reading

Eidelson, Steward G. "Spinal Column: An Integral Part of the Human Body." Available online. URL: http://www.spineuniverse.com/displayarticle.php/article2000.html. Accessed November 13, 2009. Eidelson, of South Palm Orthospine Institute, discusses the structure of the spine and explains some spinal disorders.

Hathaway, Lee, and Mrs. Buckley. "Analysis of the Anatomy and Physiology of the Chicken in Comparison to the Human," November 19, 2004. Available online. URL: http://www.duke.edu/~lah30/Work/HS%20Anatomy%20-%20Analysis%20of%20the%20Anatomy%20and%20Physiology%20of%20the%20Chicken.doc. Accessed November 13, 2009. Hathaway and Buckley discuss the value of using chickens in the study of human anatomy.

"The Vertebral Column and Spinal Cord," Anatomy Manual. Available online. URL: http://www.emory.edu/ANATOMY/AnatomyManual/back.html. Accessed November 13, 2009. Provided as notes in human anatomy, this Web site from Emory University contains extensive information on the spinal cord.

17. What Factors Affect Blood Pressure?

Topic

Blood pressure is affected by posture and activity.

Introduction

The pressure exerted by moving blood against the wall of blood vessels is known as *blood pressure*. Ventricular contraction sends blood surging into the large vessels leaving the heart. This blood is under pressure, and it causes the walls of the vessels to expand. Because it moves down a concentration gradient, blood travels from an area of high pressure just outside the heart, to an area of low pressure, a vessel. Because the heart is a pump that contracts then relaxes, blood surges into the vessels with each contraction and slows down during the relaxation phase. As a result, blood pressure alternately increases and decreases with each heart beat. For blood to flow continuously through the body, vessels must be very elastic, able to expand and recoil to their original shape. Blood pressure decreases with distance from the heart, reaching zero in the vessels that return blood into the organ.

Blood pressure is measured with a *sphygmomanometer* or blood pressure cuff. Two measurements are made. The *systolic pressure* is taken at the peak of ventricular contraction, when blood is pushed with the greatest force. *Diastolic pressure* is measured when the ventricles are relaxed. The sphygmomanometer measures blood pressure in millimeters of mercury (mm Hg). In this experiment, you will measure blood pressure in different situations to learn the effects of posture and activity.

Time Required

40 minutes

Materials

- sphygmomanometer
- stethoscope

- alcohol swabs

- science notebook

Safety Note   Do not leave the blood pressure cuff inflated around
the arm for more than a minute. Do not perform step 5c (jogging) if you
have health conditions that prevent you from participating in vigorous
physical activity. Please review and follow the safety guidelines at the
beginning of this volume.

Procedure

1. Answer Analysis questions 1 through 3.

2. Work in a group of three. Designate one member of the group as the
    subject, one as the operator, and one as the recorder.

3. The operator will find the subject's baseline blood pressure using a
    stethoscope and sphygmomanometer. To do so:

    a. Clean the earpieces of the stethoscope with alcohol.

    b. Press out any air in the blood pressure cuff.

    c. Have the subject sit comfortably with his or her right arm resting
        on a table or desk top (see Figure 1).

    d. Wrap the cuff around the arm, just above the elbow. If the cuff
        has an arrow, line it up over the brachial artery (on the inside of
        the arm). Secure the cuff so that it is snug but not tight.

    e. Gently press two fingers to the brachial artery to find the pulse.
        Place the diaphragm of the stethoscope on the brachial pulse.

    f. Pump up the cuff to about 160 mm Hg. At this pressure, the
        artery is compressed and blood cannot flow through it.

    g. Turn the pressure gauge to slowly release air from the cuff,
        listening through the stethoscope as you do. When you hear
        the first sounds, note the pressure on the sphygmomanometer
        and ask the recorder to write it in your science notebook as
        the systolic pressure. These are the sounds of blood spurting
        through the artery.

    h. Continue releasing air from the cuff, listening as you do so. You
        will notice that the sounds get louder, then they become muffled.
        When the sounds disappear, read the pressure. Have the recorder
        write this in your science notebook as the diastolic pressure.

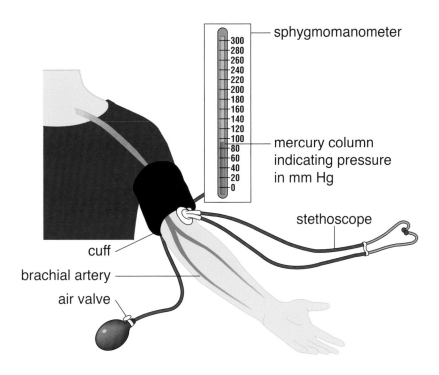

Figure 1

4. Repeat step 3 two more times to get a total of three readings. Average all three systolic pressures and all three diastolic pressures. This average is the subject's baseline blood pressure. Record the average on the data table.

Data Table		
	Blood Pressure	
	Systolic	**Diastolic**
Sitting (baseline)		
Lying down		
Standing		
Jogging		

5. Test the subject's blood pressure under the following conditions:
    a. lying down (after 2 or 3 minutes)
    b. standing (after 2 or 3 minutes)
    c. after jogging in place for 3 minutes

    As in step 3, take three readings for each condition and find an average to record on the data table.

6. Answer Analysis questions 4 and 5.

Analysis

1. Define systolic blood pressure and diastolic blood pressure.

2. Would you expect a subject's blood pressure to be higher when he or she is standing or sitting? Explain your answer.

3. Would you expect a subject's blood pressure to be higher before or after exercise? Explain your answer.

4. How did your findings in this experiment compare to your answers to Analysis questions 2 and 3?

5. What effect do you think the following would have on blood pressure? Indicate increase by "I" and decrease with "D."
    a. increased diameter of arteries
    b. increased volume of blood leaving heart
    c. severe bleeding
    d. arteriosclerosis (a condition in which arteries are partially blocked)
    e. increased pulse rate

What's Going On?

Blood pressure is directly related to two factors: cardiac output, the amount of blood pumped out of the left ventricle, and peripheral resistance, the amount of friction blood encounters as it flows through vessels. Cardiac output increases dramatically when the body's cells need extra oxygen, as in intense exercise. Factors that increase peripheral resistance include anything that narrows blood vessels such as *atherosclerosis,* a condition in which fatty deposits block, or partially block, the flow of blood (see Figure 2). The sympathetic nervous system can also narrow vessels as part of the body's *negative feedback system,* which maintains normal blood pressure. For example, if the body is not receiving enough oxygen, *vasoconstriction* occurs and blood pressure increases to speed the flow of blood to tissues. Vasoconstriction also takes place in response to cold temperature to prevent loss of body heat to the environment. In addition, the kidneys play a role in blood pressure by regulating the amount of water in blood. If blood pressure increases above normal, the kidneys remove water and dispose of it as urine. If blood pressure drops, the kidneys conserve water to increase blood volume. Chemicals can also affect blood pressure. Stimulants such as amphetamine and cocaine increase heart rate and blood pressure. Alcohol and other depressants reduce blood pressure.

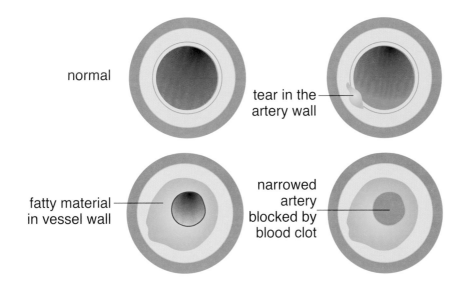

normal

tear in the artery wall

fatty material in vessel wall

narrowed artery blocked by blood clot

Figure 2

Cross sections of arteries

Connections

Normal adult blood systolic pressure varies from 110 to 140 mm Hg, and diastolic pressure ranges from 70 to 80 mm Hg. Blood pressure varies with time of day, activity, and posture. Low blood pressure, *hypotension*, can be found in conditioned athletes whose hearts beat very efficiently. The elderly may experience temporary low blood pressure when they stand, causing dizziness. Long-term hypotension that cannot be explained by physical fitness may be due to poor nutrition. Sudden onset of hypotension is a symptom of *circulatory shock*, a condition in which not enough blood is traveling through the vessels to fill them. Circulatory shock can be caused by blood loss.

Hypertension, or high blood pressure, is a common condition caused by resistance in the peripheral arteries. Known as the "silent killer," hypertension may not cause symptoms for 15 years. During this time, the heart has to pump harder to push blood through a increasing resistance. Eventually, the heart is damaged and the muscles lose some of their strength. Blood vessels are also injured as the blood creates small rips in the linings of the vessels. This process can speed the development of atherosclerosis.

Want to Know More?

See appendix for Our Findings.

Further Reading

Beevers, Gareth, Gregory Y. H. Lip, and Eoin O'Brien. "Blood pressure measurement." Adapted from *ABC of Hypertension*, 4th ed. (Hoboken, NJ: Wiley, 2001). Available online. URL: http://www.ncbi.nlm.nih.gov/pmc/articles/PMC1120141/. Accessed November 2, 2009. The authors discuss techniques for taking blood pressure and explain factors that affect blood pressure measurement.

Pesic, Milos. "Diastolic High Blood Pressure Taken Seriously," 2009. Ezine Articles. Available online. URL: http://ezinearticles.com/?Diastolic-High-Blood-Pressure-Taken-Seriously&id=562957. Accessed November 2, 2009. This article explains why a high diastolic blood pressure is dangerous.

"What Are High Blood Pressure and Prehypertension?" November 2008. National Heart Blood and Lung Institute. Available online. URL: http://www.nhlbi.nih.gov/hbp/hbp/whathbp.htm. Accessed November 2, 2009. The causes of treatments of hypertension are explained on this Web site.

18. The Integumentary System

Topic

The integumentary system has many components including skin, hair, nails, and glands.

Introduction

The skin is your largest organ, weighing 8 to 9 pounds (lbs)(3.6 to 4 kilograms [kg]) in an average adult. When you look at a person sitting near you, most of the skin that you see is dead. However, the deep layers of skin are very much alive and busy. Some of the skin's functions include the following:

- ✔ Protection. Your skin is your body's first line of defense from the outside environment. It serves as a biochemical layer and protects the inside of your body from bacteria and chemicals that may be found outside your body.

- ✔ Waterproofing. A protein in skin called *keratin* makes it waterproof. This keeps out unwanted water and conserves water within tissues to prevent desiccation.

- ✔ Temperature Regulation. Regulation of body temperature occurs in several ways. Skin acts as an insulator to maintain a proper temperature. When you are hot, skin produces sweat, a liquid that cools your body as it evaporates.

- ✔ Excretion. Some chemicals that may be dangerous to your body can be excreted through the skin. Many of these chemicals are nitrogenous wastes similar to those in urine.

- ✔ Synthesis. Your skin makes *vitamin D* when it is exposed to sunlight. Vitamin D helps bones absorb and use calcium.

- ✔ Sensory Information. Scattered throughout your skin are several types of sensory nerves that help you feel things. The sense of touch is the only sense that is not found exclusively on the head.

Your skin has varying degrees of vascularity. The outermost layer, or *epidermis*, is *avascular*, meaning it does not have any blood vessels in it.

For this reason, a scratch to the epidermis does not cause bleeding. The inner layer of skin, or *dermis*, is well vascularized and has sufficient blood flow to maintain healthy tissue. Nutrients from the dermis *diffuse* into the epidermis and support cells in that layer as well. If you have ever cut through your epidermis you may have noticed it did not bleed.

When skin is damaged, it can rapidly repair itself through the process of *regeneration,* cell division in which identical cells produced by *mitosis* can heal the damaged areas. More severe or deeper wounds, however, may take a different path called *fibrogenesis*. Instead of making new skin cells to replace the damaged cells, scar tissue is formed. The smaller the cut, the more likely it is that regeneration will take place. When you have a deep wound, stitches may be needed to pull the skin together and promote regeneration.

Glands are also a part of the integumentary system (see Figure 1). There are two main types of glands: *Apocrine glands*, or sweat glands, secrete water, *electrolytes*, and *metabolic wastes* onto the surface of the skin, and *sebaceous glands*, or oil glands, secrete an oily substance that lubricates skin and hair and kills bacteria. This keeps hair from becoming brittle and the skin from becoming dry and chapped.

Hair grows from shafts or *follicles* in the skin. Coarse hairs are located on the head and eyebrows, in the pubic region, and on the arms and legs of males. Fine hairs are found on the bodies of females, adolescents, and children. The nails on your fingers and toes also come from skin cells. Like the outer layer of the epidermis, hair and nails are made up of dead cells. That is why you can cut your hair and file your nails without bleeding and pain. In this experiment, you will examine some of the structures in your skin.

Time Required

45 minutes

Materials

- microscope
- slide
- cover slip

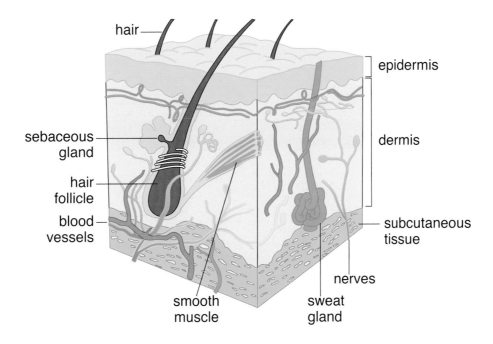

Figure 1

- pipette
- water
- petri dish
- iodine tincture
- white computer paper
- scissors
- tape
- raw chicken leg with skin
- scalpel or scissors
- sewing needle
- fishing line
- science notebook

Safety Note Iodine will stain your skin and clothes. Disinfect your lab area and wash your hands when you are finished with the chicken. Take care when using the scalpel. Please review and follow the safety guidelines at the beginning of this volume.

Procedure

1. Press your finger against the bottom of a petri dish while looking through the top of the dish. Observe any color change in your finger. Answer Analysis question 1.

2. Place a drop of iodine tincture on the bottom of the palm of your hand (near the heel of your hand). Spread it around an area about 1 inch (in.)(2.5 centimeters [cm]) square.

3. Repeat step 2, but place the iodine tincture on your wrist where a watch band would be.

4. While the iodine tincture is drying, cut two rectangles of white computer paper about the same size as the areas of iodine. After the iodine is completely dry, tape the paper over the iodine so it securely touches the skin.

5. Keep the paper on for 5 to 6 minutes (min). During this time proceed to the next step (keep track of your time). After 5 to 6 min have passed, count the number of purple dots that appear on the paper. Iodine is usually brown or gold, but when it contacts starch, it turns purple. As you sweat, the sweat transfers iodine to the paper, which contains starch, creating purple dots. The size of a purple dot indicates the activity of a sweat gland. Answer Analysis question 2.

6. Pull a piece of hair from your head (or find a piece of hair in your brush or comb). Be sure to get a hair with the root still attached to it.

7. Make a wet mount of the hair root and part of the hair shaft. Some of the hair may hang off the slide. Examine the slide through the microscope. Answer Analysis question 3.

8. Thread the fishing line through the needle.

9. Examine the skin on the chicken leg. Notice how it is attached to the tissue below. Feel of the skin and note its texture. Answer Analysis questions 4.

10. Make an incision in the skin of the chicken leg using the scalpel. Try to cut only the skin and not the muscle.

11. Use the needle and fishing line to sew up the incision you just made.

12. Repeat the process in a few more areas of the chicken leg to practice. Answer Analysis questions 5 and 6.

Analysis

1. Why did the color of your finger change when you applied pressure to the petri dish?

2. Do you have more sweat glands on the palms of your hands or on your wrists?

3. With the naked eye, hair looks smooth. What does hair look like with the microscope? Infer why the hair looks the way it does.

4. Describe the texture and appearance of the skin in your science notebook.

5. Compare the way skin heals when you get stitches with the way it heals when you do not get stitches.

6. Explain at least two ways your skin works with other body systems.

What's Going On?

If you were to examine microscopically some of the skin scraped off of your arm, you would see dead skin cells. The only living cells that are visible on a person are those that make up the lips and the eyeballs. In fact, people shed so many dead cells that dead skin is the main component of household dust. As each of us goes through our day, we leave behind a trail of dead skin cells. This trail of skin makes it possible for a trained dog to follow our paths.

In the deeper layers of skin, cells are alive, dividing, synthesizing proteins, and carrying out other life activities. One of the important proteins made deep in skin is *melanin*, a dark pigment that gives skin color. Melanin accumulates in areas forming freckles and gives moles their color. The amount of our melanin in our skin is one of the factors that makes all of us unique.

Connections

Since skin cells are constantly being shed, the deeper layers are dividing rapidly to provide replacements. Mechanisms in cells keep them from dividing unless new cells are needed. When these mechanisms fail, the cells continue to divide and grow with no regulation, a condition known as *cancer*. Cancer often forms a mass of cells like a bump or lump in the tissues. If the cell division is not stopped, the growth can continue and the cancer can spread into the lymph vessels that carry fluids throughout the body (see Figure 2).

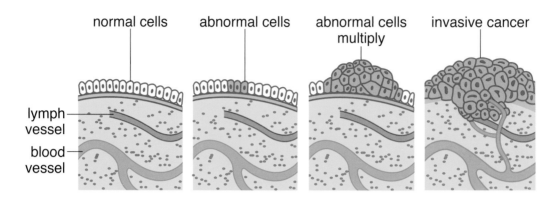

Figure 2

In order to stop the growth of these cells a person may go through *chemotherapy*, a regime of medication that kills rapidly dividing cells. One problem with chemotherapy is that the medicine cannot distinguish between good cell division and bad cell division. As a result, other rapidly dividing cells are damaged including cells in the integumentary system. Because of the stress and damage to your skin cells, people undergoing chemotherapy often lose their hair.

Further Reading

Cotterill, Simon. *Medical Terminology and Cancer,* "5: The Integumentary System (Skin)," 2001. Available online. URL: http://www.cancerindex. org/medterm/medtm5.htm. Accessed November 7, 2009. This Web page discusses the layers and functions of the integumentary system, reviews applicable medical terminology, and various cancers of the skin.

Pichay, Oliver. "Diseases of the Integumentary System," Student Nurses Community, Nursingcrib.com. Available online. URL: http://nursingcrib. com/diseases-of-integumentary-system. Accessed November 7, 2009. This Web site has information on various skin diseases from acne to warts.

"Skin (Integumentary System)," Body Guide, Adam.com, 2001. Available online. URL: http://www.mercksource.com/ppdocs/us/ cns/content/adam/visualbody/reftext/html/skin_sys_fin.html#derm. Accessed November 7, 2009. This Web page reviews the layers of the integumentary system, the two main types of sweat glands, hair, nails, and skin color.

19. Meissner's Corpuscles in Skin

Topic

Meissner's corpuscles are tactile receptors in the skin that are sensitive to light touch.

Introduction

The skin, or integument, is a complex organ made up of two regions: the outermost *epidermis* and the inner *dermis*. The epidermis is composed of several layers or strata. Moving from the bottom layer to the top, these are the stratum basale, stratum spinosum, stratum granulosum, stratum lucidum, and stratum corneum (Figure 1). Beneath the epidermis, the dermis is folded into fingerlike sections called *papillae*, which cause ridges in the epidermis above.

Because the skin covers the body, we think of it as a protective organ, but it does much more. Skin also insulates and cushions structures beneath

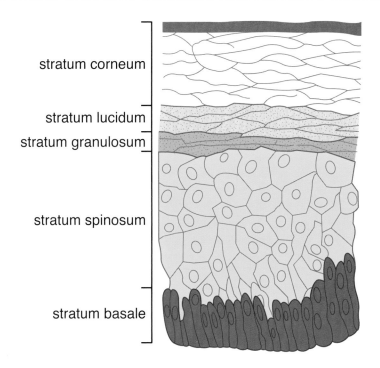

Figure 1

Layers of the epidermis

it, helps regulate body temperature, gets rid of waste products, and works with the nervous system to sense touch, pressure, pain, and heat. One kind of touch receptor is the Meissner's corpuscle, a group of nerves wrapped in a capsule, that can detect light touch (momentary contact) (see Figure 2). Meissner's corpuscles are located just below epidermis at the point where the dermis forms the papillae (see Figure 3).

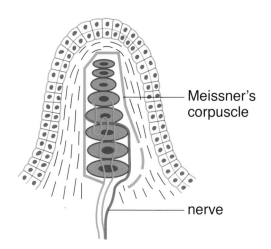

Figure 2

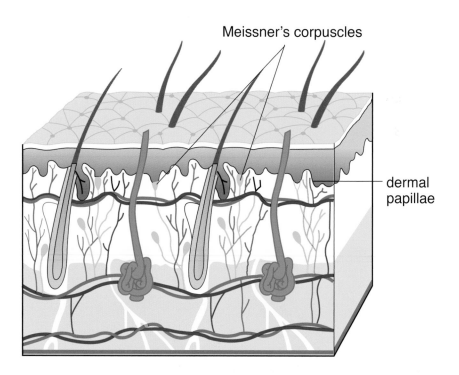

Figure 3

Meissner's corpuscles are small, encapsulated sensory structures located beneath the dermal papillae.

Structurally, each Meissner's corpuscle is made up of irregular layers of flattened cells. Nerve fibers enter the corpuscle from one side of the capsule. Inside the capsule, these nerve fibers lose their *myelin sheath*, a fatty coating that speeds transmission of nerve impulses, and the naked nerve fibers lie adjacent to the layers of cells. When the layers of cells are deformed by the slightest touch to the skin, the nerves are stimulated and send signals to the brain. In this experiment, you will examine dermal papillae and determine where on the skin they are densest.

Time Required

55 minutes for Part A
55 minutes for Part B

Materials

- compound light microscope
- prepared slide of skin with Meissner's corpuscle
- prepared slide of skin showing layers of epidermis and dermis
- washable black felt-tip pen
- washable colored felt-tip pen
- small metric ruler
- science notebook

Safety Note   Please review and follow the safety guidelines at the beginning of this volume.

Procedure, Part A

1. Use the compound light microscope to examine the prepared slide of skin. View the slide on medium power. Locate the following layers: stratum corneum, stratum lucidum, stratum granulosum, stratum basale, and dermis. Draw and label the layers of skin in your science notebook.

2. Use the compound light microscope to examine the prepared slide of skin that contains Meissner's corpuscles. Locate one corpuscle on

low power and sketch it in your science notebook. Switch to medium or high power and sketch the corpuscle at this magnification.

3. Answer Analysis questions 1 through 3.

4. Work with a partner to measure your tactile localization, your ability to tell what area has been touched. This ability depends on the density of Meissner's corpuscles in an area. To do so:

   a. One person will be the subject and the other the tester. With the subject's eyes closed, the tester touches the subject's palm with a washable black felt-tip pen. Without opening his or her eyes, the subject then tries to touch the same spot with a washable colored felt-tip pen.

   b. The tester measures the distance between the black spots and the colored spot in millimeters (ml) and records the distance in the science notebook.

   c. The tester repeats the test on the palm two more times, for a total of three trials.

   d. The tester averages the results and record them on Data Table 1 under Subject 1.

   e. Repeat steps a through d for the fingertips, ventral forearm, and back of neck.

   f. On the data table, circle the body area that has the smallest measurement. This is the region that is most sensitive to light touch and the area with the highest density of Meissner's corpuscles.

5. Tester and subject exchange roles and repeat the test. Record the results on Data Table 1 under subject 2.

6. Answer Analysis questions 4 through 7.

Data Table 1		
Region	**Measurements (ml)**	
	Subject 1	**Subject 2**
Palm of hand		
Fingertips		
Ventral forearm		
Back of neck		

Procedure, Part B

1. Design an experiment to find out which group has the densest arrangement of Meissner's corpuscles on the fingertips: males or females.

2. Before you conduct your experiment, decide exactly what you are going to do. Write the steps you plan to take (your experimental procedure) and the materials you plan to use (materials list) on Data Table 2. Show your procedure and materials list to the teacher to find out if the procedure is acceptable and if the materials you want to use are available. If you get teacher approval, proceed with your experiment. If not, modify your work and show it to your teacher again. While designing the experiment, keep these points in mind:

    a. The more individuals in your sample, the more accurate your findings.

    b. When testing individuals, work in the same region of the fingertips on each subject.

    c. Control for all variables such as temperature, the amount of pressure applied to the skin, and the type of instrument used to apply pressure.

3. Once you have teacher approval, assemble the materials you need and begin your procedure.

4. Collect your results on a data table of your own design.

Analysis

1. Meissner's corpuscles are nerve endings that are encapsulated. Other sensory structures in skin are referred to as "free nerve endings." How would you define *encapsulated*?

2. What are the layers of the epidermis?

3. Where in the epidermis are Meissner's corpuscles located?

4. Describe the appearance of the Meissner's corpuscles under the microscope.

5. What body area, palm of hand, fingertips, ventral forearm, or back of neck was most sensitive for subject 1? For subject 2?

6. When designing your own experiment, why is it important to have a large sample size?

7. What did you conclude from your experiment?

Data Table 2	
Your experimental procedure	
Your materials list	
Teacher's approval	

What's Going On?

Meissner's corpuscles are responsible for detecting light touch. The greater the density of corpuscles in an area, the more sensitive that area is to touch. In humans, some of the most sensitive areas are on the face, lips, palms of the hand, and genitals.

The distribution and number of Meissner's corpuscles in males and females is about the same. In part B, you most likely found little difference in the responses of the genders to any tactile test on the finger tips. If experimental procedures were extremely accurate, you may have found that males are slightly less able to identify the point of touch. This is because males have larger fingers than females, so their touch receptors are spread out over a larger area and are not quite as dense.

Connections

The skin contains a variety of sensory receptors. Meissner's corpuscles are one of several types of *mechanoreceptors* that perceive pain, pressure, texture, and vibrations. The others are Merkel's disks, Ruffini's corpuscles, and Pacinian corpuscles. Like Meissner's corpuscles, Merkel's disks are found near the surface of the skin and are most common in skin that is not hairy like the lips, face, tongue and finger tips. Ruffini's and Pacinian corpuscles are deeper in the tissue, near muscles and joints. These receptors are sensitive to vibrations that travel along the skeletal system, stretching of muscles and skin, and rotation of the joints.

The skin also contains thermoreceptors, which perceive sensations related to temperature. Thermoreceptors, located in the dermis, can be cold receptors or hot receptors. Cold receptors perceive cold when the temperature of an object touching the skin drops below 95 degrees Fahrenheit (°F) (35 degrees Celsius [°C]). These receptors are most stimulated at 77°F (25°C), but no longer detect cold below 41°F (5°C). That is why your hands go numb when they get very cold. Hot receptors begin to function above 86°F (30°C) and are most active at 113°F (45°C). Above this temperature, pain receptors are stimulated. Pain receptors are found in skin, muscles, some organs, and blood vessels. A sharp pain is a signal to move quickly away from the source of the pain. Dull pain is a reminder than a region has been injured and it needs to be rested until it heals.

Further Reading

Childs, Gwen V. "Touch and Position Sensory Receptors," June 4, 2001. Available online. URL: http://www.cytochemistry.net/microanatomy/nerve/touch_and_position_receptors.htm. Accessed November 11, 2009. Childs provides microscopic images of sense receptors, including Meissner's corpuscles.

DocStoc. "Interactions Between Neurons: Receptors, Synaptic Transmission and Neurotransmitters," 2010. Available online. URL: http://www.docstoc.com/docs/10772893/Interactions-Between-Neurons-

Receptors-Synaptic-Transmission-and-Neurotransmitters. Accessed May 18, 2010. This Web site provides detailed, general information on skin receptors.

Horwitz, Rick. "The Integument-Structure and Function," December 2, 2003. Available online. URL: http://www.med-ed.virginia.edu/public/ CourseSitesDocs/CellandTissueStructure/handouts/unrestricted/ original/MMHndt_Skin.html. Accessed June 2, 2010. Posted by Horwitz, of the University of Virginia, this outline on the integument provides basic information on the skin.

Science News. "Protein Tether Linked to Touch Perception," February 20, 2010. Available online. URL: http://www.sciencedaily.com/ releases/2010/100218102454.htm. Accessed March 20, 2010. Research has shown how ion channels play a role in the perception of touch.

Uzwiak, Dana. "Meissner's Corpuscles." Available online. URL: http:// bio.rutgers.edu/~gb102/lab_5/104bm.html. Accessed November 3, 2009. This virtual lab experience provides information and photographs of microscope slides of various cellular structures, including Meissner's corpuscles.

20. Model of the Digestive System

Topic

The structures of the digestive system can be represented in a model.

Introduction

The digestive system is in charge of taking in and assimilating food so that it can be used by cells. Waste products in food are also the responsibility of this system. The bulk of the digestive system is the *alimentary canal*, which extends from the mouth to the rectum. The oral cavity is the area where food is taken in, chewed, and mixed with saliva. With the help of the tongue, the slippery ball of chewed food, the *bolus*, is eased through the *pharynx* and into the muscular esophagus. Through the action of *peristalsis*, regular muscular contractions, the bolus is pushed along the esophagus toward the stomach. A *sphincter* at the end of the esophagus is usually closed to keep out stomach acid. When a bolus reaches the sphincter, the valve opens to permit entry into the stomach.

The stomach is a temporary storage structure, a wide, C-shaped tube that can stretch. When filled, the stomach can hold about 1/2 gallon (gal) (4 liters [L]) of food and liquid. The organ has three primary regions: the fundus, the body, and the antrum (see Figure 1). Within the stomach, the bolus of food is churned and mixed with strong hydrochloric acid and digestive enzymes. The partially digested mixture of broken-down food and stomach secretions is called *chyme*. This pasty, semifluid material enters the small intestine through another sphincter.

The small intestine gets its name from the fact that is has a narrow diameter, about 1 inch (in.) (2.5 centimeters [cm]) wide. However, it is the longest part of the digestive system. Within this long, thin tube, digestion is completed and nutrients and water are absorbed. The inner surface of the small intestine is lined in tiny projections called *villi* on which are found even smaller projections, the *microvilli*. These folds increase the surface area of the organ, speeding food absorption.

The last major segment of the digestive system is the large intestine or colon, a wide tube that is shorter than the small intestine. Within the

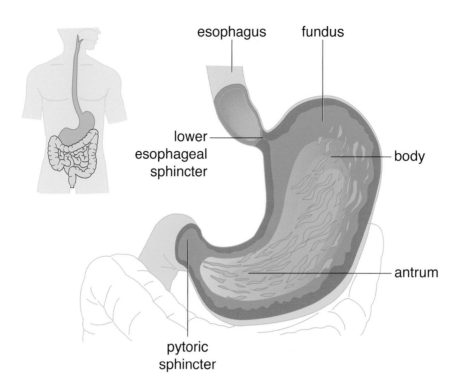

esophagus   fundus

lower
esophageal
sphincter

body

antrum

pytoric
sphincter

Figure 1

colon, water remaining in the waste is reabsorbed into the body. Dietary fiber cannot be digested, so it is one of the materials in the colon. Billions of bacteria feed on the fiber, converting some of the waste into useful materials like B vitamins and amino acids that are absorbed. Eventually, *feces,* the dried, indigestible material, is eliminated through the rectum.

As food makes its way through the alimentary canal, secretions from the accessory organs, the pancreas and liver, are added to assist in digestion. In this experiment, you will create a model of the digestive system to show the parts of the alimentary canal and the accessory organs.

Time Required

55 minutes

Materials

- clay or Play-Doh™ in 6 or 7 different colors
- plastic knife

- piece of cardboard (about the size of a desktop)
- labels
- waterproof markers
- access to anatomy book or the Internet
- science notebook

Safety Note Please review and follow the safety guidelines at the beginning of this volume.

Procedure

1. Answer Analysis question 1.
2. In an anatomy book or on the Internet, view a diagram of the digestive system. Notice the structures of the digestive system and their positions.
3. With your laboratory group, discuss and design a model of the digestive system using the materials available. Your model must show the following structures:

oral cavity	liver
tongue	pancreas
salivary glands	small intestine
pharynx	large intestine
esophagus	appendix
stomach	

4. As you are designing the model, keep these points in mind:
   a. In real life, the esophagus and the stomach are each about 12 in. (30 cm) long.
   b. The small intestine is about 25 feet (ft) (7.6 meters [m]) long.
   c. The large intestine is about 5 ft (1.5 m) long.
5. Sketch and describe your design in your science notebook.
6. Make your model on a large piece of cardboard.
7. Label each of the structures on your model.
8. Answer Analysis questions 2 through 6.

Analysis

1. Define *digestion* in your own words.

2. Compare and contrast chemical digestion and mechanical digestion.

3. Describe the jobs of the following structures:

   a. tongue

   b. salivary glands

   c. esophagus

   d. stomach

   e. liver

   f. pancreas

   g. small intestine

   h. large intestine

4. Why do the small intestines contain villi and microvilli?

5. Label the parts of the digestive system in Figure 2.

6. What might be the consequences of having an abnormally short small intestine? Explain your reasoning.

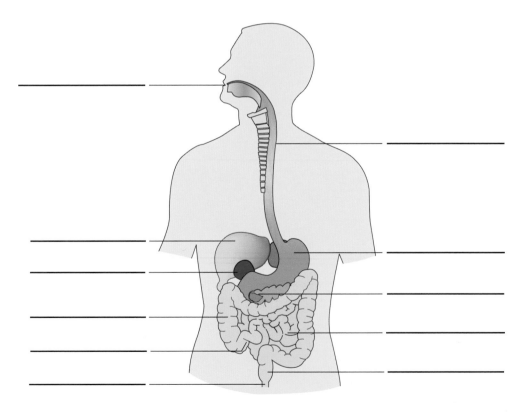

Figure 2

What's Going On?

The alimentary canal is essentially one long tube that includes the mouth, esophagus, stomach, small intestine, and large intestine. Along this tube are two important accessory organs, the liver and pancreas (see Figure 3). The liver, the largest organ in the body, has several important jobs including *detoxification*, processing nutrients, and manufacturing bile. The function of bile is to break up large globules of fat to facilitate digestion. Although bile is manufactured in the liver, it is stored in the gall bladder until needed.

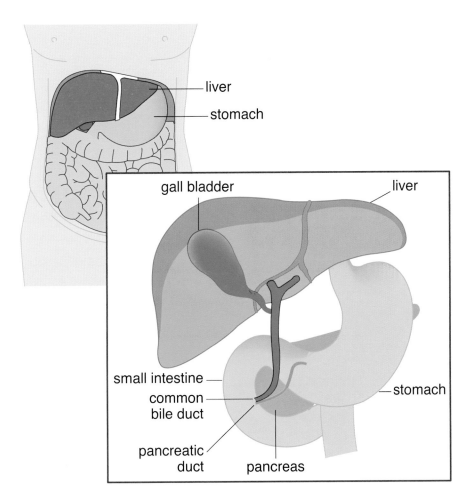

Figure 3

The pancreas is much smaller than the liver, only about 6 in. (15 cm) long. Pancreatic cells produce several types of digestive enzymes, which are collectively known as pancreatic juice. The pancreatic duct delivers these products to the small intestine. The juice is extremely alkaline to neutralize the acid produced by the stomach.

Connections

The time that food spends in the digestive system depends on several factors, including the type of food consumed. In general, 2 to 6 hours are needed to process food to its point of absorption in the small intestine. Undigested material moves to the large intestine where it stays about 72 hours. During this time, water is removed. Carbohydrates pass through the digestive system quickly; proteins take a little longer; fats take the longest.

Hormones regulate the work of the digestive system. Most of the hormones are produced by cells lining the stomach and small intestine and released into the blood stream. After circulating through the body, the hormones return to the digestive system. Here they stimulate production of digestive juices and contraction of the smooth muscles of the alimentary canal.

Three hormones that regulate the release of digestive chemicals are *gastrin*, *secretin*, and *cholecystokinin* (CCK). Gastrin triggers the production of acid in the stomach. Secretin stimulates the pancreas to release alkaline pancreatic juices, the stomach to make *pepsin*, an enzyme that breaks down protein, and the liver to release bile. Pancreatic juice production is also elicited by the release of CCK. Two other hormones tell the body when it is hungry and when its has had enough to eat. *Ghrelin*, made in stomach and upper intestine when food is not present, causes hunger. *Peptide YY* is released when food is present to suppress appetite.

Further Reading

"The Human Digestive System." Available online. URL: http://www.tvdsb. on.ca/westmin/science/sbi3a1/digest/digdiag.htm. Accessed November 11, 2009. As you mouse over the parts of the digestive system, each region is highlighted and named.

Johnson, D. R. "Introductory Anatomy: Digestive System." Available online. URL: http://www.leeds.ac.uk/chb/lectures/anatomy8.html. Accessed November 11, 2009. Dr. Johnson, provides notes on the digestive system, as well as other body systems, on the University of Leeds Web site.

"Your Digestive System and How It Works," NIH Publication 08-2681, April 2008. National Institute of Diabetes and Digestive and Kidney Diseases, National Institutes of Health. Available online. URL: http:// digestive.niddk.nih.gov/ddiseases/pubs/yrdd/. Accessed November 11, 2009. This Web site explains how food is digested and how your body regulates food intake.

Scope and Sequence Chart

This chart aligns the experiments in this book with some of the National Science Content Standards. (These experiments do not address every national science standard.) Please refer to your local and state content standards for additional information. As always, adult supervision is recommended and discretion should be used in selecting experiments appropriate to each age group or to individual students.

Standard	Grades 5–8	Grades 9–12
Physical Science		
Properties and changes of properties in matter		
Chemical reactions	6, 7, 10	6, 7, 10
Motions and forces		
Transfer of energy and interactions of energy and matter		
Conservation of energy and increase in disorder		
Life Science		
Cells and structure and function in living systems	all	all
Reproduction and heredity	14, 15	14, 15
Regulation and behavior	11	11

Standard	Grades 5–8	Grades 9–12
Populations and ecosystems		
Diversity and adaptations of organisms		
Interdependence of organisms		
Matter, energy, and organization in living systems	1, 6	1, 6
Biological evolution		
Earth Science		
Structure and energy in the Earth system		
Geochemical cycles		
Origin and evolution of the Earth system		
Origin and evolution of the universe		
Earth in the solar system		
Nature of Science		
Science in history		
Science as an endeavor	all	all

Grade Level

Title of Experiment	Grade Level
1. Tissues in the Human Body	6–12
2. External Anatomy of the Fetal Pig	6–12
3. Bone and Cartilage Structure	6–12
4. Model of the Heart	6–12
5. Dissection of a Cow's Eye	6–12
6. Food Analysis	6–12
7. Urinalysis	6–12
8. Osmosis in Red Blood Cells	9–12
9. Types of Muscles	6–12
10. Lactose Intolerance	6–12
11. Reaction Time	6–12
12. Diagnosis of Blood Diseases	6–9
13. Exercise, Pulse, and Recovery Rate	6–12
14. Male Reproductive System	6–12
15. Female Reproductive System	6–12
16. Vertebrae of the Neck	6–12
17. What Factors Affect Blood Pressure?	6–12
18. The Integumentary System	6–12
19. Meissner's Corpuscles in Skin	6–12
20. Model of the Digestive System	6–12

Setting

The experiments are classified by materials and equipment use as follows:

- Those under SCHOOL LABORATORY involve materials and equipment found only in science laboratories. Those under SCHOOL LABORATORY must be carried out there under the supervision of the teacher or another adult.

- Those under HOME involve household or everyday materials. Some of these can be done at home, but call for supervision.

SCHOOL LABORATORY

1. Tissues in the Human Body
2. External Anatomy of the Fetal Pig
3. Bone and Cartilage Structure
6. Food Analysis
7. Urinalysis
8. Osmosis in Red Blood Cells
9. Types of Muscles
14. Male Reproductive System
15. Female Reproductive System
18. The Integumentary System
19. Meissner's Corpuscles in Skin

HOME

4. Model of the Heart
5. Dissection of the Cow's Eye
10. Lactose Intolerance
11. Reaction Time

Our Findings

1. TISSUES IN THE HUMAN BODY

Idea for class discussion: Have pairs of students brainstorm their own definitions of *tissues* and *organs*. List some of the definitions on the board. After the experiment, give students an opportunity to edit the definitions if needed.

Analysis

1. Unlike skeletal muscles, cardiac muscle is branched, and there are clearly visible junctions between individual cells.

2. Sample completed data table is shown below.

Data Table			
Muscle tissue type	**Striated or unstriated?**	**Voluntary or involuntary?**	**Example of location in body**
Skeletal	striated	voluntary	biceps muscle
Smooth	unstriated	involuntary	muscle in stomach
Cardiac	striated	involuntary	heart

3. No; the shapes vary from round to lobed.

4. Answers will vary; the section of spinal cord is shaped somewhat like a butterfly. The inner and outer regions are different shades.

5. epithelial

6. a. iv; b. ii; c. vi; d. v; e. i; f. iii; g. vii; h. viii

2. EXTERNAL ANATOMY OF THE FETAL PIG

Idea for class discussion: Ask students to suggest some reasons for using fetal pigs in the study of human anatomy. Lead them to understand that pigs and humans have very similar structures.

Analysis

1. Answers will vary. Female pigs have genital papillae and males do not.

2. Answers will vary. Some pigs have pink skin; others are pigmented.

3. Answers will vary. The number of teeth depends on the age of the pig. Most will have small canines.

4. yes

5. nose

6. Pigs (both males and females) have six to nine pairs of mammary papillae.

7. a. anterior; b. dorsal; c. posterior; d. ventral. e. ventral

3. BONE AND CARTILAGE STRUCTURE

Idea for class discussion: Write the term *skeletal system* on the board and draw a circle around it. Extend several lines from the circle, drawing a spider graphic organizer. Have students fill in the lines with terms that relate to the skeletal system. After the experiment, have students add more lines and terms (in a different color).

Analysis

1. Compact bone is dense and arranged around central canals. Spongy bone is not as dense, has many open spaces, and lacks central canals.

2. Cartilage is found between bones, in the external ears, at the ends of ribs, and between vertebrae.

3. Answers will vary. The cartilage may be white or have a blue tint.

4. a. thin tissue lining the medullary cavity; b. yellow, fatty material; c. dense bone; d. thin tissue covering the bone.

5. Answers will vary. The endosteum and periosteum may no longer be visible. The marrow changes color and consistency. The compact bone changes very little.

6. The boiled bone is easier to break because some of the proteins in the tissue have been destroyed.

7. Answers will vary. All cartilage contains a lot of matrix and a few lacunae scattered throughout. In fibrocartilage, bands of collagen may be visible, and the cells may be lined up in rows between the bands. In elastic and hyaline cartilage, cells tend to be in clusters.

4. MODEL OF THE HEART

Idea for class discussion: Review the structure of the heart as a pump, pointing out the systemic and pulmonary circulations.

Analysis

1. The atria receive blood. The ventricles pump blood.

2. The tricuspid valve has three flaps.

3. The bicuspid or mitral valve has two flaps.

4. The pulmonary semilunar valve is between the right ventricle and the pulmonary artery. It prevents blood from flowing from the artery back into the ventricle.

5. The aortic semilunar valve is between the left ventricle and the aorta. It prevents blood from flowing from the aorta back into the ventricle.

6. Blood travels from the lungs to the left atrium of the heart through the pulmonary veins. It then flows into the left ventricle, from which it is pumped through the aorta to tissues all over the body. Blood returns to the right atrium of heart through the superior and inferior venae cavae. It flows into the right ventricle, and then is pumped into the pulmonary trunk, the pulmonary arteries, then to the lungs.

7. The coronary circulation delivers blood to heart tissue.

8. Blood entering the pulmonary arteries is going to the lungs. It has been to the body tissues where it gave up its oxygen.

9. The two pulmonary arteries branch off of the pulmonary trunk; one artery carries blood to the left lung; the other to the right lung.

10. The pulmonary veins deliver blood to the left atrium. This blood has been to the lungs.

11. Two veins come from each lung.

12. the head region

13. the lower body region

14. The two atria are both receiving chambers.

15. The two ventricles are both pumping chambers.

5. DISSECTION OF A COW'S EYE

Idea for class discussion: Discuss the structure of the human eye, reviewing the locations and functions of major structures.

Analysis

1. a. protective outer covering made of connective tissue; b. transparent region of the sclera in the front of the eye; c. opening through which light enters the eye; d. pigmented muscle that controls the size of the pupil; e. vascular layer of the eye that composes the retina; f. layer of light-sensitive cells in the back of the eye; g. carrier of electrical impulses from the retina to the occipital lobe of the brain.

2. Answers will vary. The cornea is cloudy and most of the eyeball is covered with fat.

3. aqueous humor

4. vitreous humor

5. Answers will vary, but the iris is dark in color and has a folded appearance.

6. The lens acts as a magnifying glass, making the print appear larger.

7. The layer is shiny and appears bright blueor silvery.

6. FOOD ANALYSIS

Idea for class discussion: Ask students to list the four major macromolecules (lipids, proteins, carbohydrates, and nucleic acids). All of these, except for nucleic acids, are major components of our diets. Have students name foods that are primarily lipid, protein, and carbohydrate in nature.

Notes to the teacher: Collect 10 food items. You will need enough of each item to give each lab group a sample about the size of a penny. Try to select foods from all food groups.

Analysis

1. carbohydrates, fats, and proteins

2. by eating a balanced diet of foods from all of the major food groups

3. The minor nutrients are only needed in small amounts.

4. Answers will vary depending on the food provided.

5. plants

6. Answers will vary but could include animal fats, coconut oil, egg yolk, meat, and vegetable oils.

7. Answers will vary but could include meat, eggs, milk, legumes (e.g., beans, peas, peanuts), nuts, and grains.

8. Answers will vary. The mechanical and chemical breakdown of food releases the nutrients, which are absorbed into the blood stream.

7. URINALYSIS

Idea for class discussion: Ask students what a medical practitioner might learn from a urinalysis. (Some students may have provided urine samples at school for random drug testing.) Point out that urine is made from blood, so it contains many of the substances that make their ways to the blood stream.

Notes to the teacher: To prepare simulated urine samples, first make a liter (L) of "normal urine" from water and yellow food coloring. Then divide the liter into six containers for whole-class use. Label the containers 1 through 6.

Container 1: Add enough baking soda to the solution to make it 3 basic. Stir well.

Container 2: Add a small amount of raw egg white and several drops of glucose. Stir well.

Container 3: Add a small amount of raw egg white. Stir well.

Container 4: Add a small amount of raw egg white. Stir well.

Container 5: Add 1 or 2 tsp of NaCl. Stir well.

Container 6: Normal urine; do not add anything to it.

Sample completed Data Table 2, is shown on page 145.

Analysis

1. Patient 1, kidney stones; Patient 2, diabetes; Patient 3, autoimmune (lupus) disorder; Patient 4, infection; Patient 5, too much aspirin; Patient 6, normal.

2. Patient 6

3. Glucose in urine, diabetes, causes a patient to be thirsty and to produce a lot of urine.

4. Answers may vary based on students' previous knowledge. The sediment is from oxalate in green plants.

5. to conserve water; in cases where enough water was not available

6. a. Ketones are from the breakdown of fat in his body. b. Answers will vary. Tissue can be damaged by such drastic weight loss. In addition, body chemistry can be altered.

Data Table 2						
Urine Sample	pH	Chloride ion	Glucose	Protein	Volume (L/d)	Blood or sediment
1	high				0.9 (low)	X
2	normal		X	X	3.3 (high)	
3	normal			X	normal	
4	normal			X	normal	X
5	high	X			low normal	
6	normal				normal	

8. OSMOSIS IN RED BLOOD CELLS

Idea for class discussion: Review the concepts of osmosis, diffusion, and concentration gradients. Ask students if they have ever been given IV "fluids." Point out that these fluids must be isotonic to blood.

Notes to the teacher: You can purchase physiological saline at the pharmacy or vet's office, or you can make a solution of 0.9 percent saline. To do so, dissolve 9 grams (g) NaCl in 700 milliliters (ml) deionized or distilled water. Add water to bring the solution volume to 1,000 ml.

To make a saltwater solution, you can simply stir several teaspoons of salt in 1,000 ml of deionized or distilled water and stir to mix. If you prefer, you can make a 2.5 percent solution, which is similar to seawater.

Analysis

1. Answers will vary. a. Water will flow into the cells. b. Water will flow out of the cells. c. There will be no net flow of water into and out of cells.

2. a. no; b. yes; from right to left

3. Distilled water caused cells to swell and salt water caused cells to shrink. In physiological saline, cells maintained the shape.

4. Blood cells will lose water and shrivel because the concentration of water is greater inside the cells than outside the cells.

5. Sample completed data table is shown at the top of page 146.

Data Table 2

	Concentration of solute in cells (low or high)	Concentration of solute surrounding cells (low or high)	Direction in which water molecules move (into or out of cells)
Hypotonic solution	high	low	in
Hypertonic solution	low	high	out
Isotonic solution	equal	equal	no net movement of water

9. TYPES OF MUSCLES

Idea for class discussion: Ask students what type of tissue they are eating when they consume a chicken breast or a steak. Discuss the fact that most of the meat we consume is skeletal muscle.

Analysis

1. Answers will vary.
2. Sample completed table is shown below.

Data Table

Characteristic	Skeletal muscle	Cardiac muscle	Smooth muscle
General shape	elongated	squarish, branched	spindle shaped
Striated or not	striated	striated	nonstriated
Voluntary or involuntary	voluntary	involuntary	involuntary
Easily fatigued or can sustain long contractions	easily fatigued	long contractions	long contractions
Location in the body	attached to bones	heart	organ and blood vessels

3. In skeletal muscle and cardiac muscle, the nucleus is found on the inner edge of the cell. This allows more space in the center of the cell for the contracting filaments that move the muscle. The nucleus in smooth muscle cells, however, is found in the center of the cell because smooth muscle cells do not need the extra space in the center of the cell.

4. Cardiac muscles must contract constantly to maintain blood flow through the body. Smooth muscles must also work continuously to keep foods and liquids moving through the stomach and intestines. Skeletal muscles do not need to maintain a constant contraction. They do, however, need to have strong bursts of contraction necessary to move an arm or pick up an object. The fibers in the skeletal muscles are arranged in a manner to allow these forceful movements, but they tire quickly.

5. The long fibers of the skeletal muscles allow for significant contraction of the individual muscle fibers or cells. The cardiac muscles are also long with intercalated disks (special junctions between their cells) that help synchronize their contractions. They are branched to improve their communication and durability around the heart. The smaller shape of smooth muscle is more conducive to squeezing smaller tubes than pulling on bones or squeezing a larger heart.

10. LACTOSE INTOLERANCE

Idea for class discussion: Find out if any of the students are lactose intolerant. Ask some to share their symptoms. If students are shy about discussing cramping and gas, point out that symptoms vary but include gastric discomfort.

Notes to the teacher: Make a glucose solution by dissolve 2 grams (g) of glucose in 70 milliliter (ml) of deionized or distilled water. Add water to the solution to 100 ml.

Analysis

1. Answers will vary based on milk products available.

2. Answers will vary. All of the milk products should contain glucose after the addition of lactase.

3. Lactase is an enzyme that helps convert lactose into simple sugars.

4. Answers will vary.

5. Enzymes function only when they are able to maintain their three-dimensional structure. Heat (as well as acids and changes in salinity) disrupt the structure of proteins.

11. REACTION TIME

Idea for class discussion: Take a vote to see how many students think we need a law prohibiting talking on the cell phone while driving. Find out how many would support a law that prohibits texting while driving. Ask them to explain their reasons.

Analysis

1. Answers will vary but could include noise, music, or texting on a cell phone.

2. Answers will vary depending on students' experimental plans.

3. Answers will vary depending on students' results.

4. If the "catcher" knows when the meterstick will fall, you are not measuring the reaction time.

5. Answers will vary depending on experimental results.

6. Answers will vary.

12. DIAGNOSIS OF BLOOD DISEASES

Idea for class discussion: Have students list some blood diseases. This may be a short list that the class can add to after the experiment.

Note to teacher: Sample completed data table for the procedure is shown on page 149.

Analysis

1. Erythrocytes carry oxygen. Hemoglobin gives them their red color.

2. Leukocytes protect the body from viruses and bacteria.

3. Answers will vary. The leukocyte count would be higher than normal because the body would be launching an attack on the viruses or bacteria causing the illness.

4. Answers will vary. Platelets enable the blood to clot, so a person with an abnormally low platelet count might be bleeding uncontrollably.

5. In both conditions, erythrocyte levels are low.

6. The erythrocytes are fragmented.

7. Answers will vary. Blood moves sluggishly through the vessels, and some areas of the body might not receive enough blood, causing pain.

Data Table					
Slide	**Erythrocytes**	**Leukocytes**	**Platelets**	**Case History**	**Diagnosis**
1	49	3	4	NA	Normal
2	40	3	1	E	Thrombotic purpura
3	36	3	4	A	Iron deficiency anemia
4	73	5	8	D	Polycythemia vera
5	33	6	4	F	Leukemia
6	38	3	4	B	Sickle cell anemia
7	51	3	9	C	Excessive clotting disorder

13. EXERCISE, PULSE, AND RECOVERY RATE

Idea for class discussion: Ask students how physical conditioning might affect recovery of normal heart rate after exercise. Have them defend their answers.

Analysis

1. A pulse is caused by the expansion of an artery when blood from the heart is pumped into it.

2. Answers will vary. Pulse is stronger at the wrist because it is nearer the heart. The strength of pulse decreases with distance from the heart.

3. Answers will vary based on experimental results.

4. Answers will vary based on experimental results.

5. *Recovery time* is the time it takes the pulse to return to normal after exercise.

6. Answers will vary. An athlete has faster recovery time because his or her heart is more efficient at pumping blood.

14. MALE REPRODUCTIVE SYSTEM

Idea for class discussion: Review the concepts of mitosis and meiosis. Ask students to explain why human gametes must be haploid.

Analysis

1. 46; 23

2. meiosis

3. Spermatogonia are the germ cells that will produce sperm. They are located within the seminiferous tubules, close to the basement membrane.

4. Answers will vary. Sperm are streamlined so that they can travel to the egg.

5. Most sperm are long and thin with a bullet-shaped head, a midpiece, and a long taillike flagellum. Deformed sperm may have abnormalities such as short tails, two tails, or no tail. In some cases, the head of the sperm is round or unusually small.

15. FEMALE REPRODUCTIVE SYSTEM

Idea for class discussion: Review the differences in male and female gamete production.

Analysis

1. epithelial cells

2. A primary follicle is made up of an oocyte that is surrounded by two layers of granular cells.

3. A graafian oocyte is relatively large and contains a fluid-filled cavity.

4. The corpus luteum produces estrogen and progesterone, which maintain the uterus for pregnancy.

5. The ovaries of a 40-year-old woman have been producing corpus lutea for years; the scars show the sites of these corpus lutea.

6. The vaginal mucosa is made of several layers of epithelial cells and topped with squamous cells.

16. VERTEBRAE OF THE NECK

Idea for class discussion: Have students feel the vertebrae in the back of their necks. Start with the largest one (C7), which is at the base of the neck. Have them count upward to see how many vertebrae they can palpate. (There are 7 cervical vertebrae.)

Analysis

1. Answers will vary due to butchering techniques, but there should be between 12 and 14.

2. Vertebrae provide a bony protection that keeps the spinal cord from being damaged.

3. Sample completed figure below.

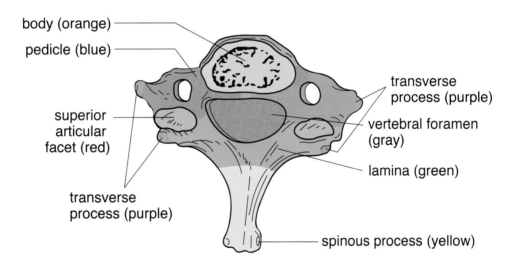

4. Muscles attach to the body of the vertebrae and to the processes.

5. Vertebrae attach on the superior and inferior articular processes.

6. Answers will vary. Individual vertebrae vary in size and shape.

17. WHAT FACTORS AFFECT BLOOD PRESSURE?

Idea for class discussion: Ask how many students know if they have "normal," high, or low blood pressure. Discuss with them how they found out this information.

Analysis

1. Systolic pressure occurs when the ventricles contract; diastolic pressure occurs when the ventricles relax.

2. Answers will vary. Blood pressure drops upon standing, then increases slightly. After a long period of standing, the blood pressure may drop even more.

3. Answers will vary. Blood pressure is higher after exercise because the heart is working harder.

4. Answers will vary.

5. a. D; b. I; c. D; d. I; e. I

18. THE INTEGUMENTARY SYSTEM

Idea for class discussion: Have students look at their fingertips with a magnifying glass and describe what they see. If they magnifiers are very good quality, they may see the openings of sweat glands. The ridges are caused by dermal papillae. Have them compare their fingertips to the backs of their hands.

Analysis

1. The pressure pushes the blood away from the area touching the petri dish. The blood leaves the skin, creating a lighter skin appearance.

2. There are more sweat glands on the palms of your hands than on the wrists.

3. The hair looks flaky and layered. This is because layers of cells are added to the hair as it grows.

4. Answers will vary.

5. Answers will vary. If you got stitches, the skin is closer together and the wound is smaller. The skin would undergo regeneration and heal the wound with skin cells. If you did not get it stitched up, fibrogenesis would occur and create scar tissue.

6. Answers will vary, but may include the following:

    Skeletal system: the skin makes vitamin D to help our bodies to absorb calcium and make strong bones.

    Immune system: the skin protects the body from foreign substances and acts as a barrier.

    Nervous system: the skin has sensory receptors for touch.

    Excretory system: the skin rids the body of potentially toxic substances.

19. MEISSNER'S CORPUSCLES IN SKIN

Idea for class discussion: Ask students if they have ever had a tiny insect on their skin and did not even know it. Point out that for us to feel an insect on our skin, it has to move, triggering our sensory receptors. An insect that is holding still might escape our notice.

Analysis

1. Answers will vary. *Encapsulated* means to be encased in a protective membrane.

2. stratum basale, stratum spinosum, stratum granulosum, stratum lucidum, stratum corneum

3. Meissner's corpuscles are located between the stratum granulosum and stratum lucidum (at the dermal papillae).

4. Answers will vary based on observations.

5. Answers will vary based on experimental results.

6. Answers will vary. A large sample size reduces the impact of those rare individuals who have unusual responses.

7. Answers will vary based on experimental results. Males and females have the same number of Meissner's corpuscles in the skin of their fingers. However, males have larger fingers, so their corpuscles are spread over a larger area. Therefore, the skin on their fingers is a little less sensitive than the skin on female's fingers.

20. MODEL OF THE DIGESTIVE SYSTEM

Idea for class discussion: Ask students how medical practitioners visualize the digestive system. Discuss endoscopy and colonoscopy, MRIs, and CT scans.

Analysis

1. Answers will vary but should include converting the complex molecules of food into simple molecules that the body can absorb.

2. Answers will vary. Chemical digestion involves the breaking up of food with enzymes and acids. Mechanical digestion refers to tearing and churning food.

3. a. mixes food and pushes it to the back of the throat; b. produce saliva, which contains enzymes and moistens food; c. connects pharynx to stomach; d. churns and squeezes food and mixes it with enzyme and acids; e. provides bile; f. provides digestive enzymes;

g. complete digestion and absorbs nutrients; h. absorbs water and stores wastes.

4. Villi and microvilli increase surface area, making it possible for the small intestine to absorb all of the nutrients.

5. See sample completed figure below.

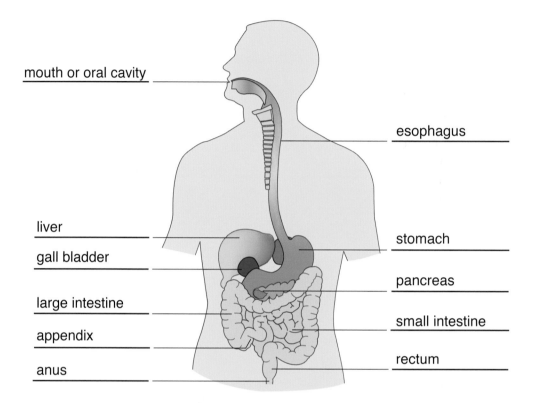

mouth or oral cavity

esophagus

liver

gall bladder

stomach

pancreas

large intestine

small intestine

appendix

rectum

anus

6. Answers will vary. With an abnormally short small intestine, a person might not be able to digest food completely or absorb all of the nutrients. As a result, the individual could be small for his or her age or malnourished.

Glossary

acrosome structure on the head of the sperm that contains enzymes

adenosine triphosphate (ATP) molecule made up of adenosine, ribose, and three phosphate groups that carries energy in the cell

alimentary canal muscular tube of the digestive tract, beginning with the mouth and ending at the anus that is lined with mucous membranes

anemia a medical condition due to either a reduced number of red blood cells or lack of hemoglobin, the oxygen-carrying molecule within erythrocytes

antrum a cavity or opening in bone

apical surface the upper surface of an epithelial cell

aplastic anemia type of anemia caused by insufficient production of red blood cells by the bone marrow

apocrine gland sweat gland in skin that secretes water and metabolic waste products

aqueous fluid clear fluid in the eyeball between the cornea and the lens

artery vessel that carries blood away from the heart to tissues in the body

atrium upper chamber of the heart that receives blood

autonomic nervous system part of the nervous system that controls involuntary actions, such as contraction of heart and smooth muscle and secretion of glands

avascular lacking blood vessels

axial skeleton section of the skeletal system that includes the skull, vertebrae, and rib cage

basal surface the lower portion of an epithelial cell

basophil type of white blood cell involved in inflammation

biceps brachii muscle in the upper arm, raises the forearm when contracted

bladder part of the urinary system that stores urine

blood pressure measure of the force that blood exerts against the arterial wall

blood smear a microscope slide made from a small drop of blood spread across the slide so that cells are separated for easy examination

bolus mass of food that has been chewed and mixed with saliva

Bowman's capsule in the kidney, a cuplike sac that surrounds the glomerulus and functions in filtration

brachialis muscle in the upper arm situated just deep of the biceps brachii that helps raise the lower arm

bradycardia the condition of having a heart beat slower than 60 beats per minute

canaliculi small canal connecting lacunae in compact bone

cancer a group of diseases caused by abnormal cell division

cardiac muscle involuntary, striated muscle that makes up the walls of the heart

cellular respiration   process in which oxygen is used to change glucose into energy for cellular use

centrum   central or main portion of a vertebra

cholecystokinin (CCK)   hormone that stimulates the digestion of lipids and proteins

chondrocyte   cartilage cell that produces and secretes the matrix in which it lives

chyme   partially digested food that moves from the stomach into the small intestine

cilia   tiny, hair-like projections of the cell membrane of some cells that help move materials along the cell's surface or provide a method of locomotion in single-cell organisms

ciliary body   ring of muscle fibers that holds the eye's lens in place and helps regulate pressure within the eye

circulatory shock   serious medical condition in which there is not enough blood in circulation to support all tissues

cone   type of light-sensitive cell in the retina that perceives color

conjunctiva   membrane that lines the eye socket and covers the eye

cornea   transparent covering of the eye that refracts light

coronary circulation   the circulation of blood in the blood vessels that provides blood to heart muscle

coronary sinus   vessel in the coronary circulation that carries blood to the right atrium

coronary sulcus   groove on the heart that separates the atria from the ventricles

corpus luteum   a hormone-secreting, yellow mass of cells formed from an ovarian follicle that has ruptured

creatine kinase an enzyme found in high concentrations in heart and skeletal muscles

dermis layer of skin below the epidermis

detoxification   neutralization or break down of poisonous substances

diffuse   to move from an area of high concentration to an area of low concentration

disaccharide   a carbohydrate such as sucrose or lactose that is made from the combination of two simple sugars

ectoderm   in an embryo, the outer layer of tissue that develops into skin and the nervous system

elastic cartilage   type of cartilage found in outer ear and larynx that contains numerous elastic fibers

electrolyte   substance such as chloride, calcium, or phosphate that can conduct electricity when dissolved

endoderm   the inner most layer of tissue in an embryo that develops into digestive and respiratory structures

endosteum   thin layer of tissue that lines the medullary cavity of bones

eosinophils   white blood cells whose primary role is in fighting parasites

epidermis   the outer layer of skin, made of stratified squamous epithelium

epididymis   coiled tubule extending from the testis where sperm mature

erythrocytes   red blood cells, the structures that carry oxygen in the blood

estrogen   female sex hormone, produced by the ovary, that controls the menstrual cycle and is responsible for female secondary sex characteristics

facet   flat surface on a vertebra that articulates with the adjacent vertebra

feces   solid wastes of the digestive system that contain undigested matter, bacteria, mucus, and dead cells

fertilization   the combination of egg and sperm to produce a zygote

fibrocartilage   type of cartilage found at the ends of ribs and between vertebrae that contains collagen fibers

fibrogenesis   the development of fibrosis scar tissue

follicle   any cavity containing a small sac, such as a hair follicle or ovarian follicle

formalin   solution of formaldehyde and water used as a preservative

formed elements   red and white blood cells and platelets found in blood

fovea centralis   area in the retina made up of cones where vision is the sharpest

gamete   sex cell; sperm or egg cell

gap junction   connection between two cells that joins their cytoplasm for rapid communication

gastrin   hormone that stimulates the production of acid in the stomach and speeds up digestion

gestation   the period during which an embryo develops

ghrelin   hormone secreted by the stomach that stimulates appetite

glomerulus   loop of blood vessels in the kidney where blood is filtered and wastes are removed

gonad   organ that makes gametes

Haversian system   unit of compact bone that contains a central canal for the passage of blood vessels and nerves; also called an osteon

hematocrit   the amount of red blood cells in blood

hemoglobin   iron-containing pigment in erythrocytes that binds to oxygen

hemolysis   break down of erythrocytes that releases hemoglobin

hemolytic anemia   type of anemia in which erythrocytes undergo hemolysis and are unable to function

herniated disc   tear in the fibrocartilage of an intervertebral disc that allows the disc to put pressure on nearby nerves

histamine   chemical released by cells of the immune system that causes inflammation

hormone   chemical released by an endocrine gland that travels to a target organ where it has a specific effect

hyaline cartilage   cartilage that covers the articulating surfaces of bones and makes up most of the fetal skeleton

hypertension   condition in which blood pressure is high, over 140/90 millimeters of mercury (mm Hg)

hypertonic   of a solution on one side of a membrane having a higher concentration of solutes than on the other side of the membrane

hypotension   abnormally low blood pressure that cannot be explained by athletic conditioning

hypotonic   of a solution on one side of a membrane that has a lower concentration of solutes than the solution on the other side of the membrane

inferior vena cava   large vessel that carries blood from the lower part of the body back to the heart

intercalated disc   specialized junction between cells of cardiac muscle that allows electrical impulses to spread easily from one cell to the next

interstitial cells   cells located in the spaces between other cells

intervertebral disc   pad of fibrocartilage between two adjacent vertebrae

involuntary muscle   muscle that contracts without conscious control; smooth muscle and cardiac muscle

iris   membrane that controls the amount of light that enters the eye

isotonic   of two solutions with the same concentration of solutes

keratin   tough protein produced by skin cells that provides waterproofing

lacunae   small cavities in which cells are located

lamina   thin layer or plate, such as the laminae that make up the arch of a vertebra

lobule   a small anatomical division

lymphocyte   type of white blood cell that occurs in two types, antibody producing B lymphocytes and T lymphocytes that participate in cell-mediated immune responses

lyse   to burst or break open a cell

macula lutea   yellow depression in the center of the retina that contains the fovea centralis

mammal   an animal characterized by hair and the production of milk from mammary glands for its offspring

matrix   the material in which cells are embedded

meatus   natural body opening or canal

medullary cavity   cavity in the central shaft of long bones that contains bone marrow

meiosis   type of cell division in which the chromosome number is reduced by one half

Meissner's corpuscle   type of nerve ending in skin that is responsible for sensitivity to light touch

melanin   pigment that gives skin its color and protects DNA in skin cells from damage by ultraviolet radiation

melanocyte   type of skin cell that produces melanin

mesoderm   the middle layer of tissue that develops into muscle, bone, cartilage, and blood

microfilament   thin filament made of actin found in muscle and in the cytoskeleton of cells

microvillus   microscopic, fingerlike extension of the cell membrane that increases a cell's surface area

mitosis   type of cell division in which daughter cells are clones of the original parent cell

monocyte   type of white blood cell that consumes microbes and other foreign matter

mononucleate   having one nucleus per cell

monosaccharide   simple sugar such as glucose or fructose

multinucleate   having more than one nucleus per cell

muscle fiber   muscle cell; a contractile structure that is the basic unit of a muscle

myelin sheath   fatty covering on some nerve cells that helps speed transmission of nerve impulses

nephron   the smallest functional unit of the kidney

neutrophil   type of white blood cell that consumes cell debris and foreign material to fight infection

nictitating membrane   protective, inner membrane that covers the eye in birds, reptiles, and some mammals

nutrient   chemical compound such as water, carbohydrates, lipids, and proteins that an organism needs to sustain life

omnivore   animal that feeds on plants and other animals

oocyte   a female gamete; an egg cell

oogenesis   production of a female gamete

oogonia   diploid cell that gives rise to the haploid female gamete

optic disc   point at which the optic nerve leaves the eye

osmosis   the movement of water molecules from an area of high concentration to an area of low concentration

osseous cell   a cell made up of, or related to, bone

osteon   a Haversian system, a unit of compact bone that contains a central canal for the passages of blood vessels and nerves

ovarian follicle   saclike group of cells in which an ovum develops

ovary   female gonad, the structure in which eggs cells form

oviduct   tube through which an egg cell travels from the ovary to the uterus

ovulation   the process of releasing an egg cell from a follicle

ovum   an egg cell, a female gamete

palpate   to examine an area by touch, usually with the hands

peptide YY   hormone in the small intestine that suppresses appetite

periosteum   membrane covering bone to which muscles and tendons connect

peristalsis   wavelike contractions of smooth muscle that move food along the alimentary canal

pharynx   the throat, the area between the oral cavity and the esophagus

placenta   temporary organ that connects a developing fetus to the uterus for transfer of oxygen and nutrients and removal of wastes

plasma   the straw-colored liquid part of blood

polar body   small cell produced by the uneven distribution of cytoplasm in oogenesis

primary follicle   enlarged oocyte that is surrounded by a layer of cuboidal granulosa cells

primordial follicle   oocyte that is surrounded by a single layer of follicular epithelial cells

progesterone   female hormone produced by the ovaries that maintains the uterus for implantation of a fertilized egg

pulmonary artery   one of two vessels that branch from the pulmonary trunk to carry blood from the right ventricle to the lungs

pulmonary circulation   part of the cardiovascular system that carries deoxygenated blood from the heart to the lungs and oxygenated blood from the lungs back to the heart for circulation through the body

pulmonary trunk   main vessel that carries blood from the right ventricle; the pulmonary trunk branches into the right and left pulmonary arteries

pulmonary vein   one of four veins that carry oxygenated blood from the lungs to the left atrium

pulse   regular expansion and contraction of arteries with each heart beat

pupil   adjustable opening in the iris of the eye through which light enters

purpura   purplish splotches caused by bleeding under the skin

regeneration   regrowth of tissue that is damaged or lost

renal tubule   small tube in the nephron that leads away from the glomerulus where materials filtered from blood become urine

retina   light-sensitive membrane on the back of the eye that is connected to the optic nerve

rod   type of light-sensitive cell in the retina that perceives objects in dim light

saturated fat   type of lipid primarily found in animal products that has a single covalent bond between carbon atoms; typically solid at room temperature

sclera   protective white tissue that covers the outside of the eyeball

scrotum   external sac of skin that holds the testes

sebaceous gland   gland in the skin that produces sebum

secondary follicle   oocyte that has an antrum and is surrounded by multiple layers of cells

secretin   hormone produced by the small intestine that neutralizes acids and slows digestion

selectively permeable membrane   type of membrane that permits the passage of only some substances

semen   fluid produced by the male reproductive system that contains sperm

seminiferous tubules   tiny, coiled tubes within the testis in which sperm are produced

septum   tissue that separates two cavities or areas

Sertoli cell   type of cell found in the testis that provides nutrients and hormones that support developing sperm

sickle cell anemia   inherited disease of the blood in which some erythrocytes form rigid, sickle shapes that cause circulatory problems

skeletal muscle   voluntary, striated muscle that is connected to bone

smooth muscle   involuntary, unstriated muscle found in organs and blood vessels

spermatid   immature sperm cell produced by spermiogenesis

spermatocyte   diploid cell that undergoes meiosis to produce four haploid spermatids

spermatogenesis   series of cell divisions in the testes that lead to the production of sperm

spermatogonia   cells that are precursors to sperm

spermatozoa   sperm; the reproductive cell of males

spermiogenesis   the final stages of spermatogenesis in which spermatids develop into mature sperm

sphincter   ring of muscle that contracts or relaxes to regulate the passage of materials

sphygmomanometer   instrument with an inflatable armband that is used to measure blood pressure

spinous process   bony projection from the back of a vertebra to which muscles attach

spongy bone   open, meshlike bone tissue found at the ends of long bones and in the center of other types of bone

striation   strip or band found in some types of muscle tissue

superior vena cava   large vessel that carries blood from the upper part of the body back to the heart

systemic circulation part of the cardiovascular system that carries oxygenated blood from the heart to the body and deoxygenated blood from the body to the lungs

tachycardia abnormally fast heart rate

testis male gonad, the structure in which sperm cells form

tissue group of similar cells that perform a function

transverse process lateral protrusion of bone from a vertebra that serves as a point of attachment for muscles

triglyceride lipid made of three fatty acids and a glycerol

troponin an enzyme that can be measured in blood to indicate whether or not heart muscle has been damaged

ulna the long bone between the elbow and the wrist of the forearm

umbilical cord cord that connects a developing fetus to the placenta

unsaturated of a type of lipid primarily found in plant products that has one or more double bonds between carbon atoms; typically liquid at room temperature

ureter tube that carries urine from the kidney to the bladder

uvea layer of the eye beneath the sclera that contains the iris, choroid layer, and ciliary body

ventricle pumping chamber of the heart

vertebral foramen large opening in a vertebra

vesicular (Graafian) follicle a cavity in the ovary that contains a mature oocyte and is surrounded by follicular cells in which there is a fluid-filled cavity

vestigial structure nonfunctional structure, such as the appendix, that may have been functional in an ancestral form

villus small projection on a mucus membrane

vitreous humor clear fluid that fills the posterior chamber of the eyeball

voluntary muscle skeletal muscle that can be contracted at will

zygote diploid cell formed by the fusion of an egg and a sperm

Internet Resources

The World Wide Web is an invaluable source of information for students, teachers, and parents. The following list is intended to help you get started exploring educational sites that relate to the book. It is just a sample of the Web material that is available to you. All of these sites were accessible as of June 2010.

Educational Resources

"Anatomy of The Eye," 2009. Macula.org. Available online. URL: http://www.macula.org/anatomy/. Accessed November 15, 2009. Images and a video of the eye's interior on this Web site explain eye structures and their functions.

Bianco, Carl. "How Your Heart Works," 2009. howstuffworks. Available online. URL: http://www.howstuffworks.com/heart.htm. Accessed November 15, 2009. Images and information on the heart and how it works are explained simply on this Web page.

Dye, Lee. "Why Cell Phones and Driving Don't Mix," June 29, 2005. ABC News Technology & Science. Available online. URL: http://abcnews.go.com/Technology/DyeHard/story?id=889064&page=1. Accessed May 17, 2010. This article explains how one researcher came to the conclusion that people are not able to concentrate on a task when they are listening to someone talk.

"Epithelial Tissues," 2009. Human Anatomy & Physiology, Biology 201 Laboratory Materials, MESA Community College. Available online. URL: http://www.mc.maricopa.edu/~minckley/anatomy/epithelial_tissue.html. Accessed November 15, 2009. This Web site provides excellent views of epithelial tissues.

Fleck, Earl W. "Virtual Pig Dissection," Biology Department, Whitman College. Available online. URL: http://www.whitman.edu/biology/vpd/. Accessed November 15, 2009. This Web site gives students views of fetal pig anatomy and describes structures.

"Heart Valve Disease," 2009. WebMD. Available online. URL: http://www.webmd.com/heart-disease/guide/heart-valve-disease. Accessed November 15, 2009. Mitral valve prolapse and other diseases of the heart valves are explained on this Web site.

"Histology of Bone and Cartilage." University of Ottawa. Available online. URL: http://www.courseweb.uottawa.ca/medicine-histology/english/Musculoskeletal/default.htm#Cartilage. Accessed November 15, 2009. This Web site has many slides and a great deal of information on cartilage and bone tissue.

Jastrow, Holger. "Workshop Anatomy for the Internet." Available online. URL: http://www.uni-mainz.de/FB/Medizin/Anatomie/workshop/englWelcome.html. Accessed November 17, 2009. Dr. Jastrow of Johannes Gutenberg University, Mainz, Germany, shares a wealth of notes and photographs on topics of human biology.

Kahn, Charles, E. November 27, 2006. CHORUS: Collaborative Hypertext of Radiology. Available online. URL: http://chorus.rad.mcw.edu/about-CHORUS.html. Accessed November 17, 2009. This Web site is a reference for students studying anatomy and imaging.

"Lactose Intolerance," June 2009. National Digestive Diseases Information Clearinghouse. Available online. URL: http://digestive.niddk.nih.gov/ddiseases/pubs/lactoseintolerance/. Accessed November 15, 2009. The causes, symptoms, and treatment of lactose intolerance are explained on this Web site.

"Lactose Intolerance," 2004. University of Wisconsin Hospitals and Clinics. Available online. URL: http://www.uhs.wisc.edu/docs/uwhealth_lactose_177.pdf. Accessed November 17, 2009. This Web site discusses sources of lactose and alternatives for those who are intolerant.

"Map of the Human Heart," 1997. Available online. URL: NOVA.http://www.pbs.org/wgbh/nova/heart/heartmap.html. Accessed November 15, 2009. This Web site shows how blood travels through the heart.

"Muscle Tissue," Histology Department, University of Delaware. Available online. URL: http://www.udel.edu/biology/Wags/histopage/colorpage/cmu/cmu.htm. Accessed May 17, 2010. Excellent views of muscle cells, including neuromuscular junctions and intercalated discs of cardiac muscle are provided on this Web site.

"Portrait of a Cell," 2000. Colorado State University. Available online. URL: http://www.vivo.colostate.edu/hbooks/cmb/cells/index.html. Accessed November 15, 2009. Osmosis in red blood cells, plasma membranes, and the nucleus are some of the topics discussed on this Web site.

"Sickle Cell Disease," 2009. Blood Diseases, University of Maryland. Available online. URL: http://www.umm.edu/blood/sickle.htm. Accessed November 15, 2009. This Web site explains the causes and treatments of sickle cell disease.

Simerville, Jeff A., William C. Maxted, and John J. Pahira. "Urinalysis: A Comprehensive Review," 2005. *American Family Physician*. Available online. URL: http://www.aafp.org/afp/20050315/1153.html. Accessed November 15, 2009. In this article, the authors explain several types of urine tests and how to interpret their results.

"Tissues of Life," 2006. Available online. URL: http://www.smm.org/tissues/. Accessed November 15, 2009. Supported by the Science Museum of Minnesota and the National Institute of Health, this interactive Web site lets students view virtual microscopic slides of tissues.

"Urinalysis." Internet Pathology Laboratory for Medical Education. Available online. URL: http://library.med.utah.edu/WebPath/TUTORIAL/URINE/URINE.html. Accessed November 15, 2009. On this Web site, macroscopic and microscopic analyses of urine are clearly explained.

Index